AN ANALYSIS OF THE CAUSAL FACTORS BEHIND THE UNITED STATES
NAVY'S WARSHIP-BUILDING PROGRAMS FROM 1933 TO 1941

A thesis presented to the Faculty of the U.S. Army
Command and General Staff College in partial
fulfillment of the requirements for the
degree

MASTER OF MILITARY ART AND SCIENCE
Military History

by

JOHN M. BARRETT, LCDR, USN
B.S., Marquette University, Milwaukee, WI, 1991
M.S., Boston University, Boston, MA, 1999

Fort Leavenworth, Kansas
2005

Approved for public release; distribution is unlimited.

REPORT DOCUMENTATION PAGE

Form Approved
OMB No. 0704-0188

Public reporting burden for this collection of information is estimated to average 1 hour per response, including the time for reviewing instructions, searching existing data sources, gathering and maintaining the data needed, and completing and reviewing this collection of information. Send comments regarding this burden estimate or any other aspect of this collection of information, including suggestions for reducing this burden to Department of Defense, Washington Headquarters Services, Directorate for Information Operations and Reports (0704-0188), 1215 Jefferson Davis Highway, Suite 1204, Arlington, VA 22202-4302. Respondents should be aware that notwithstanding any other provision of law, no person shall be subject to any penalty for failing to comply with a collection of information if it does not display a currently valid OMB control number. **PLEASE DO NOT RETURN YOUR FORM TO THE ABOVE ADDRESS.**

1. REPORT DATE (DD-MM-YYYY)	2. REPORT TYPE	3. DATES COVERED (From - To)
17-06-2005	Master's Thesis	Aug 2004 - Jun 2005

4. TITLE AND SUBTITLE

An analysis of the causal factors behind the U.S. Navy's warship building program from 1933-1941

5a. CONTRACT NUMBER

5b. GRANT NUMBER

5c. PROGRAM ELEMENT NUMBER

6. AUTHOR(S)

LCDR John M. Barrett

5d. PROJECT NUMBER

5e. TASK NUMBER

5f. WORK UNIT NUMBER

7. PERFORMING ORGANIZATION NAME(S) AND ADDRESS(ES)
U.S. Army Command and General Staff College
ATTN: ATZL-SWD-GD
1 Reynolds Ave.
Ft. Leavenworth, KS 66027-1352

8. PERFORMING ORGANIZATION REPORT NUMBER

9. SPONSORING / MONITORING AGENCY NAME(S) AND ADDRESS(ES)

10. SPONSOR/MONITOR'S ACRONYM(S)

11. SPONSOR/MONITOR'S REPORT NUMBER(S)

12. DISTRIBUTION / AVAILABILITY STATEMENT

Approved for public release; distribution is unlimited.

13. SUPPLEMENTARY NOTES

14. ABSTRACT

On 7 December 1941, the US Navy had 343 warships in commission, however, a 'second' fleet, consisting of 344 warships, was in various stages of construction in shipyards across the country. Given that building a warship could take anywhere from less than a year for a destroyer, to over three years for a battleship or aircraft carrier, it is clear that the foresighted building of warships in the years prior to US involvement in World War II would play a major role in enabling the US Navy to counter and eventually defeat the Imperial Japanese Navy in the Pacific. In order to trace the evolving influences behind this warship building program, this thesis divides the pr-war period into three separate phases: Phase one is bounded by Roosevelt's inauguration and the *USS Panay* incident. Phase two runs from the *USS Panay* incident until the fall of France. And phase three continues from the fall of France until the attack on Pearl Harbor. In total, the building programs of all three pre-war phases amount to 586 warships.

15. SUBJECT TERMS

US Navy, warship construction, naval disarmament treaties, inter-war period, US Navy's preparedness for WWII, Navy Department.

16. SECURITY CLASSIFICATION OF:			17. LIMITATION OF ABSTRACT	18. NUMBER OF PAGES	19a. NAME OF RESPONSIBLE PERSON
a. REPORT	b. ABSTRACT	c. THIS PAGE			
Unclassified	Unclassified	Unclassified	UU	121	19b. TELEPHONE NUMBER (include area code)

Standard Form 298 (Rev. 8-98)
Prescribed by ANSI Std. Z39.18

MASTER OF MILITARY ART AND SCIENCE

THESIS APPROVAL PAGE

Name of Candidate: LCDR John Michael Barrett

Thesis Title: An Analysis of the Causal Factors Behind the United States Navy's Warship-Building Programs from 1933 to 1941

Approved by:

_____, Thesis Committee Chair
Lieutenant Colonel Marian E. Vlasak, M.A.

_____, Member
Stephen D. Coats, Ph.D.

_____, Member
David W. Christie, M.A.

Accepted this 17th day of June 2005 by:

_____, Director, Graduate Degree Programs
Robert F. Baumann, Ph.D.

The opinions and conclusions expressed herein are those of the student author and do not necessarily represent the views of the U.S. Army Command and General Staff College or any other governmental agency. (References to this study should include the foregoing statement.)

ABSTRACT

AN ANALYSIS OF THE CAUSAL FACTORS BEHIND THE UNITED STATES NAVY'S WARSHIP-BUILDING PROGRAMS FROM 1933 TO 1941 by LCDR John Michael Barrett, 121 pages.

On 7 December 1941, the US Navy had 343 warships in commission; however, a "second" fleet, consisting of 344 warships, was in various stages of construction in shipyards across the country. Given that building a warship could take anywhere from less than a year for a destroyer, to over three years for a battleship or aircraft carrier, it is clear that the foresighted building of warships in the years prior to US involvement in World War II would play a major role in enabling the US Navy to counter and eventually defeat the Imperial Japanese Navy in the Pacific. In order to trace the evolving influences behind this warship building program, this thesis divides the pr-war period into three separate phases: Phase 1 is bounded by Roosevelt's inauguration and the USS *Panay* incident, phase two runs from the USS *Panay* incident until the fall of France, and phase three covers from the fall of France until the attack on Pearl Harbor. In total, the building programs of all three prewar phases amount to 586 warships.

ACKNOWLEDGMENTS

Foremost, I wish to thank my committee chair, LTC Marian Vlasak, USA, for guiding me through this challenging project. Her mentorship and support, along with that of Dr. Stephen Coats and Mr. David Christie, played a key role in my successfully completing this thesis. Additionally, I'd like to acknowledge the assistance of the skilled research staff at the Combined Arms Research Library. They were able to facilitate the intra-library loan of several essential references, and were instrumental in assisting me to access primary source material in their collection.

TABLE OF CONTENTS

Page

MASTER OF MILITARY ART AND SCIENCE THESIS APPROVAL PAGE ii

ABSTRACT iii

ACKNOWLEDGMENTS iv

ACRONYMS vii

ILLUSTRATIONS ix

TABLES x

CHAPTER 1. INTRODUCTION 1

    Literature Review 6
    The Seeds of Naval Disarmament (1919-1920) 10
    Washington Naval Conference 13
    Geneva Conference 20
    London Naval Treaty 21
    Looking Ahead 23
    Significant Causal Factor: 1919-1932 25

CHAPTER 2. BUILDING A TREATY FLEET, 1933-1937 30

    The Process by Which Warships Are Built 35
    Warship-Building Programs, 1933-1937 37
    Causal Factors for Phase One (1933-1937) 46

CHAPTER 3. FLEET EXPANSION IN THE GATHERING STORM: 1938-1940 50

    Neutrality Acts 55
    Changes in the Navy Department 56
    Causal Factors 63

CHAPTER 4. THE SURGE IN BUILDING: A PRELUDE TO WAR, 1940-1941 67

    Expansion of the FY 1941 Building Program 70
    Naval Expansion Act of 14 June 1940 70
    New Man at the Helm: Secretary Frank Knox 71
    Naval Expansion Act of 19 July 1940 74
    Further Increases in the FY 1941 Building Program 75
    Retooling the Department of the Navy 76

Destroyers for Bases Agreement, 2 September 1940 77
Changes within the Navy 81
Europe First 82
Lend Lease Act, 11 March 1941 84
FY 1942 Building Program 85
Final Steps Toward Entering the War 86
Causal Factors 89

CHAPTER 5. SUMMARY AND CONCLUSION 93

Interpretations of the Most Significant Causal Factor for Period 1933-1941 99
Applications of Lessons Learned from the Analysis 100
Recommended Further Study 104

BIBLIOGRAPHY 106

INITIAL DISTRIBUTION LIST 109

CERTIFICATION FOR MMAS DISTRIBUTION STATEMENT 110

ACRONYMS

ADM	Admiral
BB	Battleship
BG	Brigadier General
CA	Heavy Cruiser
CAPT	Captain
CDR	Commander
CL	Light Cruiser
CNO	Chief of Naval Operations
CV	Fleet Aircraft Carrier
CVE	Escort Aircraft Carrier
D	Democrat
DD	Destroyer
DE	Destroyer Escort
ENS	Ensign
FY	Fiscal Year
GA	Georgia
GEN	General
HMS	His/Her Majesty's Ship
ID	Idaho
IJN	Imperial Japanese Navy
LCDR	Lieutenant Commander
LT	Lieutenant
LTjg	Lieutenant Junior Grade

LTG	Lieutenant General
MA	Massachusetts
MG	Major General
NIRA	National Industrial Recovery Act
R	Republican
RADM	Rear Admiral
RN	Royal Navy
SS	Submarine
UK	United Kingdom
US	United States
USN	United States Navy
USS	United States Ship
USSR	Union of Soviet Socialist Republics
VADM	Vice Admiral

ILLUSTRATIONS

	Page
Figure 1. Warships in US Navy from 1932 to 7 December 1941	2
Figure 2. Mandate Islands	34

TABLES

Page

Table 1.   United States Replacement Table 18

Table 2.   London Naval Armaments Limitation Treaty..23

Table 3.   Second London Naval Treaty Categories 44

Table 4.   US Warships on 7 December 1941 88

Table 5.   Warship Building Appropriations: 1933-1937 95

Table 6.   Warship Building Appropriations: 1938-1940 97

Table 7.   Warship Building Appropriations: 1940-1941 99

Table 8.   Warship Building Appropriations: 1933-1941 99

CHAPTER 1

INTRODUCTION

The US Navy (USN) experienced its finest hour in its defeat of the Imperial Japanese Navy (IJN) in World War II. As the major allied naval force in the Pacific, the US Navy played the key role in enabling US land forces to assault and recapture Japanese-seized islands throughout the theater. Given that building a warship could take anywhere from less than a year for a destroyer to three years or more for a battleship or aircraft carrier, it is clear the foresighted buildup of the US Navy's warships during the period of 1933 to 1941 played a critical role in the early stages of the war.

The US Navy's fleet of 7 December 1941 had its origins in the years prior to the war and as such, was constructed to meet a varying mix of economic, political, and military requirements of these prewar years. In order to facilitate the analysis of the origins and impacts of each of these causal factors, the period from 1933 through 1941 will be broken into three phases where each highlights a significant causal factor unique from the other two phases. As the analysis steps through each phase, it should become apparent that the geopolitical situation which drove the causal factors of the building program shifts as each phase is analyzed. The first phase begins in 1933 with the arrival of President Roosevelt in office and ends in 1937 with the USS *Panay* incident. The second phase of analysis begins in 1938 and runs through 1940, ending with the outbreak of war in Europe. The final phase of analysis continues from the outbreak of war in Europe through the attack on Pearl Harbor on 7 December 1941.

For the purposes of this thesis, warships are defined as: aircraft carriers, battleships, cruisers, destroyers, destroyer escorts, and submarines. Minesweepers-layers, auxiliaries, patrol craft, airships, and seaplane tenders will neither be discussed nor will they be considered in fleet composition totals, except where specifically noted.

From the arrival of President Roosevelt in office in early 1933 up until the attack on Pearl Harbor on 7 December 1941, the US Government appropriated funding for 586 warships. In terms of warships in commission, fully constructed, and serving actively with the fleet, the numbers increased from 190 in 1932 to 345 on the eve of the attack (see figure 1).

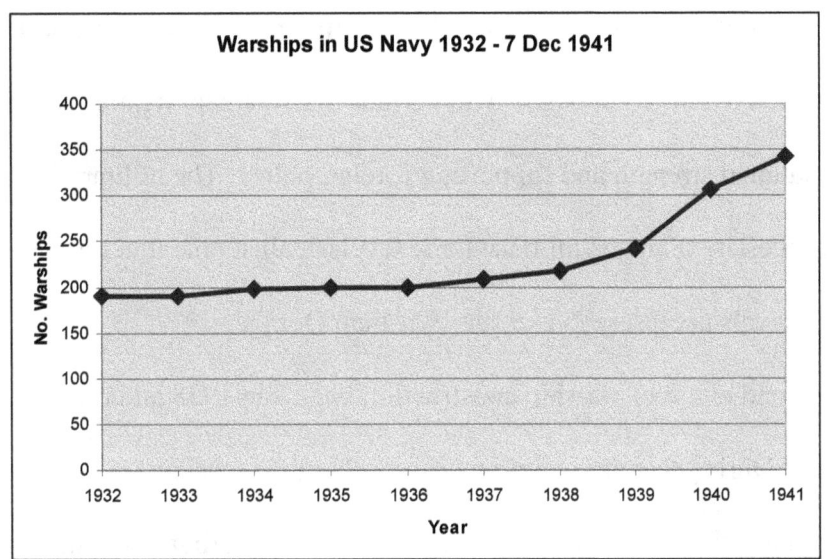

Figure 1.   Warships in US Navy from 1932 to 7 December 1941
Source: "US Navy Active Ship Force Levels, 1917-Present" [database on-line], (Washington DC: U.S. Naval Historical Center), accessed 24 September 2004; available from http://www.history.navy.mil/branches/org9-4.htm; Internet.

This thesis explores the question: What were the causal factors that led the United States to initiate this robust building and expansion program from 1933-1941? Additionally, this thesis attempts to identify the most significant of the causal factors that influenced naval construction in this era. The thesis is that the causal factors which led to this building program span a myriad of military, political, and economic issues throughout these years and can best be analyzed and understood through the identification and delineation of the three distinct phases found between 1933 and 7 December 1941.

During the first phase, which commenced with the inauguration of President Roosevelt in 1933, the Navy's building program existed primarily as a portion of his overall economic recovery strategy known as the "New Deal." As a consequence, the underlying economic influence of this phase was New Deal spending directed at the economic benefits of building warships. Political influences during this phase included the issue of directives for compliance with various disarmament treaties while maintaining national strength and supporting foreign policy. The military influences included the necessity to match military force levels against potential threats as well as required force levels necessary to execute War Plan Orange.

The second phase of warship construction begins in 1938 and runs until the fall of France in 1940. During this phase, international reliance on disarmament treaties as a means to guarantee the peace fails amid a climate of accelerating international military preparedness and rearmament. Politically, the need to ensure the nation and its allies were appropriately armed for war was a significant influence during this phase. Militarily, the principal influence on building during this period was the pressure to avoid obsolescence, while constructing up to allowable treaty limits. The principal economic influences of the phase were centered on funding the building programs as a means to stimulate the economy and maintaining the shipbuilding industry.

The third and final phase of prewar warship construction begins with the fall of France in the early summer of 1940 when the military requirement to accelerate construction of a fleet of warships supersedes the economic and political anxieties that had previous limited the scope of building in the prior years.

Chapter 1 introduces the thesis, provides a literature review, and covers relevant background material on the status and influences on US warships from the end of World War I through 1932. An analysis of the US Navy's building program starts at the end of World War I and sets the scene for events to follow, including the politics of the treaty of Versailles and the significant naval disarmament treaties of this phase including the Washington and London treaties. It concludes by selecting the principal causal factor for this phase.

Chapter 2 examines the first phase of the warship-building program covering the years from 1933 to 1937. The chapter includes an explanation of the process by which warship-building programs are originated, staffed, authorized, and appropriated. It explores in detail the building programs of the phase, as they relate to the president's New Deal economic recovery program. Additionally, it examines the origins of War Plan Orange and its development over years as influenced by treaty-governed US force levels, the expanding role of the aircraft carrier, and Japanese expansion in the Pacific. Further, the chapter analyzes important legislation and treaty regulations of the phase to include the Vinson-Trammel Act of 1934 and the Second London Naval Treaty of 1937. The chapter concludes by identifying the principal military, political, and economic causal factors of the phase and provides an assessment of their relative significance.

Chapter 3 examines the second phase of prewar building from 1938 through 1940. It looks at the growing need to increase productive capacity to meet modernization requirements of the fleet. The military, political, and economic influences of this phase are also weighed, such as the creation of the Atlantic Squadron, the weakening of the Pacific-based US Fleet and its ability to carry out an Orange campaign, the economic ability of the nation to build to treaty limits, and the gradual shift in public opinion away from isolationism. The chapter concludes by identifying the principal military, political, and economic causal factors of the phase and provides and further selects the most significant of these three.

Chapter 4 examines the final phase of the building program and covers from the fall of France in 1940 to the attack on Pearl Harbor on 7 December 1941. The clarified threats and military requirements that drove vast expanse in warship building during this phase will be examined, as well as the reduction in economic constraints and public opinion pressure that allowed it. Both Navy Expansion Acts of June and July 1940 and the expanded appropriations to the fiscal year (FY) 1941 building program are discussed. Political factors that contributed to the building program are given context through an examination of Britain's war with Germany and the US continued effort to assist without provoking involvement. Japanese aggression in the Pacific is examined for its contribution to the building programs of this phase. The chapter concludes by analyzing the principal military, political, and economic causal factors of the phase and identifies the most relatively significant of these three.

Chapter 5 provides a brief summary of the above chapters, as well as a conclusion that will justify the selection of the most significant causal factor (military, political, or economic) behind the US Navy's prewar warship-building program throughout the entire period from 1933 through 7 December 1941. Additionally, this chapter suggests areas for further study and applies the lessons from this thesis to today's Navy and its warship building program.

Literature Review

There are many sources, both primary and secondary, that provide information relevant to this thesis. Unfortunately, there are no works completely dedicated to a comprehensive study of the US Navy's pre-World War II warship-building program and its causal factors. Nonetheless, information is contained in numerous works, which address broader issues. As such, most of the available source material briefly addresses aspects of the warship-building program as it relates to the broader context of national preparedness for war. No works seems to address the subject in detail.

One particularly useful source is *Naval Policy Between the Wars* written by Stephen Roskill in 1968.[1] This work contains an exhaustive study of both the US and United Kingdom (UK) naval policies between the two world wars and pays particular attention to building programs, technological innovations, personalities involved, international treaties, and national politics as they relate to both the US and UK. He makes extensive use of primary sources, such as minutes from meetings, and provides an extensive list of source material.

Arms Limitations and Disarmament; Restraints on War, 1899-1939 edited by B. J. C. McKercher and published in 1992,[2] is extremely useful in providing analysis and insight into the treaties of the phase. The book is a compilation of chapters each written by different author and comprises an in-depth study on individual arms control treaties of the phase. It makes use of a large volume of primary-source data relevant to the treaties and provides a thorough examination of the political impacts of each agreement. His work contains an exhaustive bibliography and is a particularly useful source of further primary source material on the subject.

The treaty documents themselves, including the 1922 Washington Treaty,[3] the 1930 London Treaty,[4] and the Second London Treaty of 1936,[5] have been especially helpful in understanding their respective influence on the building programs, which followed. The text of the Destroyers for Bases Agreement,[6] the Lend Lease Act,[7] the Naval Expansion Act of 14 June 1940,[8] and the Naval Expansion Act of 19 July 1940,[9] each available through the *Statutes at Large,* have been particularly useful in providing the primary source information on the legislative impact on warship construction issues throughout the interwar period.

In analyzing the military aspects of the building program, there are several excellent references regarding War Plan Orange and other strategic topics relevant to this thesis. Edward S. Miller's *War Plan Orange,* published in 1991,[10] and Henry G. Gole's *The Road to Rainbow,*[11] published in 2003, both are comprehensive studies of the subject. They fully examine the plan from its earliest inception through the years as it is continually updated to reflect changes in strategy, technology, international treaties, and international climates. Both include thorough lists of references including many primary sources, especially government documents related to the subject. Miller's inclusion of force structure requirements necessary to execute the plan is particularly useful.

FDR and the U.S. Navy, edited by Edward J. Marolda and published in 1998,[12] provides an outstanding study on the relationship between the president and the US Navy throughout a span of almost thirty years. The work comprises a series of essays transcribed from speeches given during a conference of the same name held in 1996. The essays superbly capture the many facets of the relationship President Roosevelt maintained with "his Navy," and benefits from a variety of scholarly understanding of this complex and enduring relationship. It traces this relationship from Roosevelt's earliest association with the US Navy as the distant cousin of then-Assistant Secretary Theodore Roosevelt, through to his own appointment as Assistant Secretary in World War I, on to his rise to the presidency and his influence on the Navy throughout the years leading to World War II. It is well researched and documented to facilitate further research.

Conway's All the World's Fighting Ships 1922-1946,[13] is an outstanding reference on combat fleets of the world throughout the period of this thesis. In addition to a comprehensive listing of individual warships, a brief analysis of the annual building programs behind their construction is also included. Also, the *US Navy's Vessel Registry*[14] provides invaluable data on US warship strength throughout the period of this thesis. Further useful sources include Samuel E. Morrison's *The Two-Ocean War* published in 1963.[15] It provides an excellent summary of the US Navy's actions throughout World War II and is a very useful compendium of his larger, fifteen-volume series *The History of the United States Navy in World War II*. Additionally, *The History of the U. S. Navy,* Volume I: *1775-1941,* by Robert W. Love Jr.,[16] was the most useful overall historical summary of the US Navy during the period of this thesis. It contains an extremely comprehensive history of the broad range of issues affecting the warship-building programs throughout the years. It is very well referenced and sourced to facilitate further research.

In compiling information regarding the political influences of the building program, several works stand out including Kenneth Davis' *FDR, Into the Storm, 1937-1940*,[17] published in 1993, which includes thorough source and bibliographical information on the domestic political situation in the years leading to the war. William Leahy's *I Was There*[18] and Henry Adams' *Witness to Power*,[19] both provide superb information on and by the senior naval officers in the inner circle of the administration on the issue. Admiral Leahy's work is an invaluable reference for tracking the timing of political issues and concept development as it was written in journal form from notes and diary entries made at the time. Further useful primary source material is available through President Roosevelt's personal letters as compiled by his son Elliot Roosevelt in his 1950 work, *F.D.R. His Personal Letters, 1928-1945,* Volumes I and II.[20] Finally, Robert Dallek's *Franklin D. Roosevelt and American Foreign Policy, 1932-1945,*[21] compiles an essential study of the president's impact on US foreign policy and by extension, his impact on the Navy and its building program throughout his terms in office.

Several sources have been useful to determine the underlying economic influences on the building program. They include V.R. Cardozier's 1995 work *The Mobilization of the United Stated in World War II: How the Government, Military and Industry Prepared for War,*[22] which covers all aspects of the mobilization for war and pays particular attention to the economics of the effort. Whereas William E. Leuchtenburg's *Franklin D. Roosevelt and the New Deal, 1932-1940,*[23] does an excellent job of chronicling the New Deal throughout the Roosevelt administration. Alan

Brinkley's *The End of Reform: New Deal Liberalism in Recession and War*[24] nicely fills in the gaps by explaining in detail all of the influences which led to New Deal policy changes throughout the prewar years. Both works are extensively referenced and include thorough bibliographies.

The remainder of this introductory chapter serves to set the stage for those that follow. It will describe the relevant influences to the 1933-1941 warship-building programs by broadly examining issues from the end of World War I through 1932 that played a role in shaping events that followed. This information is not meant to provide causal factors that would compete with those that will be discussed in later chapters, but rather is included to offer background historical information so that the decisions embarked upon later can be understood in the context with which they were made. This early focus on the disarmament treaties, specifically the Treaty of Versailles, the Washington Naval Treaty, the Geneva Conference, and the London Naval Treaty, is meant to provide a sense of their residual impact on the US Navy's building program throughout the 1930s.

The Seeds of Naval Disarmament (1919-1920)

Throughout the 1920s and up until the arrival of President Roosevelt in the White House, the principal influence on US Navy warship construction was the Versailles Treaty and its subsequent generative powers with respect to the naval disarmament treaties that followed. The two most significant impacts on the building programs of the 1920s and early 1930s were the condition of the US Navy following World War I and the treaties under which warship building were to be regulated. As expressed by Samuel Elliot Morison, the US Navy's famous World War II historian, the experience of the coming war was to be nothing like that of the previous conflict. New elements of warfare, technologies, and enemies were to emerge which would transform the US Navy's understanding of war.

> Although the United States participated heavily in World War I, the nature of that participation was fundamentally different from what it became in World War II. The earlier conflict was a one-ocean war for the Navy and a one-theater war for the Army; the latter was a two-ocean war for the Navy and one of five major theaters for the Army. In both wars a vital responsibility of the Navy was escort-of-convoys and anti-submarine work, but in the 1917-1918 conflict it never clashed with the enemy on the surface; whilst between 1941 and 1945 it fought some twenty major, and countless minor engagements with the Japanese Navy. American soldiers who engaged in World War I were taken overseas in transports and landed on docks or in protected harbors; in World War II the art of amphibious warfare had to be revived and developed, since assault troops were forced to fight their way ashore. Air power in the earlier conflict was almost negligible; in the latter it was a determining factor. In World War I the battleship still reigned queen of the sea, as she had, in changing forms, since the age of Drake, and battle line fought with tactics inherited from the age of sail; but in World War II the capital naval force was the aircraft carrier task group, for which completely new tactics had to be devised.[25]

Clearly, the manner in which the US Navy used the years between World War I and World War II was of critical importance in ensuring that the fleet was adequately prepared to meet all of these changes.

As World War I ended the US Navy found itself a vastly powerful, yet unbalanced force, equipped primarily for the convoy escort and antisubmarine warfare missions of the northern Atlantic. Because of these wartime missions, the force was heavily destroyer-centric. By the time the final ships of the wartime-building program were commissioned into the fleet in 1920, a total of 267 "flush deck" destroyers were commissioned. By July of 1920, the US Navy had 300 warships in commission and 567 total ships in the fleet.[26]

President Wilson's foreign policy was centered on his conviction that through international dialog and acceptance of the rule of law, future wars could be avoided. He advocated a series of issues summarized in his fourteen points which stipulated among other things, freedom of the seas outside territorial waters, large-scale disarmament of the combatants, the resolution of former German colonial possessions, and perhaps most important, the creation of the League of Nations.[27]

With the disintegration of the German Army and the rapid self-imposed demobilization of the American and British armies, by the spring of 1919 only the French Army and the Allied Powers' navies were left as objects for international disarmament. Once the war was concluded, the British planned to reestablish the Royal Navy (RN) as master of the seas by ensuring that no armaments reduction treaty scaled down the size of their fleet, particularly in relation to that of the United States. Knowing this, just prior to the Armistice conference, President Wilson asked Congress for funding to complete the battleships authorized in the 1916 building program. His intention to use this large program as a bargaining chip with which to compel the allies into accord over his fourteen points was evident in his statement that, "I want to go to the Peace Conference armed with as many weapons as my pockets will hold so as to compel justice."[28]

Thanks to his request, work was resumed on twelve battleships: two California class, four Maryland class, and six mammoth South Dakota class. After carefully analyzing the economics of their situation, the British dropped their insistence that they alone maintain the largest postwar fleet. The US then cancelled its follow-on naval building program of 1918 and agreed to drop those ships from the 1916 program that had not yet laid down.[29] Thus the impasse between Britain and the US was broken. On 28

April 1919, the peace conference approved the revised draft of the covenant and the treaty itself was signed on 28 June 1919.

The Senate's second rejection of the treaty in 1920 led the Secretary of the Navy to request funding from Congress for an interim-building program of two battleships and one battle cruiser. Although this request was not approved by Congress, overseas, particularly in Britain, it was seen to violate the spirit if not the letter of the truce signed at Versailles Conference a few months earlier. Within the British Admiralty the US-building request strengthened lingering doubts in American good faith and increased hostility over the US' insistence of naval parity with Britain.[30] Thus as the new Harding administration took office in 1921, the US foreign policy and Wilson's attempt to influence international events through naval policy were both in disarray.[31]

Washington Naval Conference

Support for disarmament among western countries was swelling among their respective populations, politicians, and press corps. Even those traditionally supportive of maintaining naval strength were forced to admit that maintaining huge fleets was now impractical with the demise of the German fleet and no obvious European adversary left to face. Added to this was a growing suspicion in the US government of the Anglo-Japanese Alliance, which had been in force since 1902. During this period the US grew more concerned over the increasing threat to US interests in the Western Pacific posed by an increasingly militant and expanding Japanese empire. The Japanese expansion in the region, both through military conquest and assumption of German possessions following the Treaty of Versailles, posed a growing challenge to US access to China, and the sea line of communication to the Philippines and the US territory of Guam. There was growing fear in the United States Navy that a conflict with Japan over these issues in the Western Pacific would draw Great Britain in on the Japanese side.[32]

In response to these growing concerns, the Harding administration seized the initiative and invited the world's powers to an international conference that was set to convene in Washington in November 1921. As relations were beginning to strain with Great Britain and Japan, no word of the proposals to be discussed was disseminated. To the astonishment of all the attendees, Harding's Secretary of State, Charles Hughes stunned the attendees when he opened the conference with a memorable speech proposing massive cuts in the world's existing surface fleets and further specifying a plan which included exactly which ships were destined for the breakers yard. Correctly anticipating the plan's overwhelming support among the public, politicians, and the press, Secretary Hughes deviated from the cautious approach of his naval advisors and shrewdly left no alternative for the assembled delegates but to debate the specifics of the proposal.[33]

His proposals included an immediate cancellation of all existing capital shipbuilding programs, a ten-year cessation of capital shipbuilding, and the scrapping of thirty ships from the US Navy (fifteen new and fifteen old), twenty-three from the Royal Navy (four new and nineteen old), and seventeen from the Imperial Japanese Navy (seven new and ten old). If this plan were to go into effect, the US would possess eighteen capital ships (500,650 tons), the British twenty-two (604,450 tons), and the Japanese would have ten (299,700 tons).[34]

The initial tonnage limits were increased to enable the Japanese to retain the newly commissioned battleship *Matsu* and to enable Great Britain to complete construction on the recently ordered Hood class battleships, which would fill their urgent need to modernize their aging capital ship fleet. In order to match these gains, the US won concession from the other parties to allow them to retain two partially completed West Virginia class battleships, the *Colorado* and *Washington*, both scheduled for completion in 1922.[35]

Within the context of the Treaty, several important definitions were specified in order to ensure universal compliance:

> Capital Ship Defined as a vessel of war, not an aircraft carrier, whose displacement exceeds 10,000 tons (10,160 metric tons) standard displacement, or which carries guns with a caliber exceeding 8 inches (203 millimeters).
> Aircraft Carrier Defined as a vessel of war with a displacement in excess of 10,000 tons standard displacement designed for the specific and exclusive purpose of carrying aircraft. It must be so constructed that aircraft can be launched therfrom and landed theron, and not designed and constructed for carrying a more powerful armament than that allowed to it under Article IX (not more than eight guns of six inch caliber) or Article X (no aircraft carrier can carry a gun in excess of eight inch caliber), as the case may be.
> Standard Displacement Defined as the displacement of the ship complete, fully manned, engined, and equipped ready for sea, including all armament and ammunition, equipment, outfit, provisions and fresh water for crew, miscellaneous stores and implements of every description that are intended to be carried in war, but without fuel or reserve feed water on board.
> Ton Defined as 2240 pounds (1016 kilos).[36]

These definitions were critical to the eventual treaty, as well as those that followed as they gave the negotiators and their supporting naval staffs something more specific with which to negotiate and alternatively, in terms of war plans, something to work around.

Following three months of diplomatic negotiation, the Washington Treaty was signed on 6 February 1922 and was set to remain in effect through 31 December 1936. After making allowances for ships in commission and or under construction, the treaty limited capital ship tonnage to a 5:5:3:1.75:1.75 ratios for the US, Britain, Japan, France, and Italy, respectively. Using these ratios, the US and Great Britain were limited to

525,000 tons, the Japanese: 315,000 tons, and the French and Italians: 175,000 tons. The Washington Naval Treaty established a ten-year "building holiday" for all capital ships except aircraft carriers. Additionally, the treaty specifically prohibited capital ships in excess of 35,000 tons and limited capital ship armament to no more than sixteen-inch diameter. Guns on smaller warships were limited to no more than eight inches in diameter.[37]

Aircraft carriers, although also regarded as capital ships, had their maximum tonnage limits specified in a separate section of the treaty. Here again, the signatories agreed to the same capital ship ratio as applied to battleships and battle cruisers, but with differing tonnage maximums. The US and Britain were limited to 135,000 tons of aircraft carriers, Japan to 81,000 tons, and France and Italy to 60,000 tons. In addition to these maximum tonnage limits, the treaty also specified that only two carriers per country could exceed 27,000 tons, and of those two, neither could exceed 33,000 tons. As specified in the above definitions, the number of large guns an aircraft carrier could carry was also limited in order to prevent an aircraft carrying battleship from being classified as an "aircraft carrier," thus effectively increasing the number of battleships a country could maintain. Additionally, any aircraft carrier in commission at the time was deemed to be "experimental" and as such did not count against a country's allotted tonnage for that class. The US Navy's first carrier, USS *Langley,* fell under this category. With the allowable limit for aircraft carriers unfilled, two of the battle cruisers scheduled for scrapping (*Lexington* and *Saratoga*) were converted to carriers. As a specially governed category of allowable capital ship tonnage, aircraft carriers were the only capital ships that could be constructed up until 1932 when the planned capital ship-building moratorium was due to expire.[38]

A concession yielded by the US and Great Britain to the Japanese delegation in order to get them to agree to the smaller ratio of capital ships was to agree to a status quo with respect to naval bases and fortifications in the Pacific. Each nation specified exceptions to this prohibition. The US could fortify its mainland bases (including the mainland of Alaska), Hawaii, and the Panama Canal Zone. All other territories and possessions of the US, including the Aleutian Islands, the Philippines, and Guam, were prohibited from be fortified or expanded beyond that which existed at the date of signing. Britain was allowed to build and fortify on Australia and New Zealand, but not Hong Kong. Japan could fortify its home islands, but not Formosa.

The impact of the Washington Treaty on the US Navy capital ship levels and by extension, its impact on construction of replacement capital ships well into the future was specified via a replacement table in section II of the treaty. This replacement plan provided the US a schedule of ships to be scrapped or broken up prior to commissioning (in the case of those depicted with an age of zero) in order to comply with the treaty. Additionally, the schedule of replacement capital ships, planned nominally to occur at the replaced ship's twenty-year point, as well as the planed number of modern "post-Jutland" battleships in commission for each year is also depicted. Similar schedules were drawn up and included in the treaty for each country. Table 1 is the US Replacement Table taken directly from the text of the Washington Treaty.[39] It specifies allowable US Navy building from 1922 through 1942.

Table 1. United States Replacement Table					
	Ships laid down	Ships completed	Ships scrapped (age in parentheses)	Ships retained summary	
Year				Pre-Jutland	Post-Jutland
			Maine (20), Missouri (20), Virginia (17), Nebraska(17), Georgia (17), New Jersey (17), Rhode Island, (17) Connecticut (17), Louisiana (17), Vermont, (16), Kansas (16), Minnesota (16), New Hampshire, (15), South Carolina (13), Michigan (13), Washington (0), South Dakota (0), Indiana (0), Montana (0), North Carolina (0), Iowa (0), Massachusetts (0), Lexington (0), Constitution (0), Constellation (0), Saratoga (0), Ranger (0), United States (0)*	17	1
1922		A, B#	Delaware (12), North Dakota (12)	15	3
1923				15	3
1924				15	3
1925				15	3
1926				15	3
1927				15	3
1928				15	3
1929				15	3
1930				15	3
1931	C, D			15	3
1932	E, F			15	3
1933	G			15	3
1934	H, I	C, D	Florida (23), Utah (23), Wyoming (22)	12	5
1935	J	E, F	Arkansas (23), Texas (21), New York (21)	9	7
1936	K, L	G	Nevada (20), Oklahoma (20)	7	8
1937	M	H, I	Arizona (21), Pennsylvania (21)	5	10
1938	N, O	J	Mississippi (21)	4	11
1939	P, Q	K, L	New Mexico (21), Idaho (20)	2	13
1940		M	Tennessee (20)	1	14
1941		N, O	California (20), Maryland (20)	0	15
1942		P, Q	2 ships in West Virginia class	0	15

*The United States may retain the *Oregon and Illinois,* for noncombatant purposes, after complying with the provisions of Part 2, III(b).
Two West Virginia Class.
Note. A, B, C, D, etc., represent individual capital ships of 35,000 tons standard displacement, laid down and completed in the years specified.

Source: U.S. Naval Arms Limitation Treaty, 6 February 1922, *Statues at Large* (1923-1925), vol. 43, pt 2.

Ships to be decommissioned and scrapped in order to come into compliance with the treaty are listed at the top of the table with the corresponding age in years of the ship listed in parentheses. Scheduled capital ship building, represented in the table by capital letters corresponding to each ship, is specified in terms of the year construction was to commence, and the year the ship was to be completed. Those ships scheduled to be decommissioned or scrapped in order to make way in the allowable tonnage as these new ships were constructed and commissioned as also listed. If the Washington Treaty and its follow-on treaties were to remain in force, this schedule would have governed the US Navy's construction of capital ships up through 1942, and thus would have had a tremendous impact on the nation's preparedness for war.

The Washington Treaty cast a long shadow on US Navy force structure during the relatively unfettered decades leading up to World War II. Its allowance for aircraft carrier capital ship construction helped to infuse enthusiasm for naval aviation where previously there had been little. By securing British support for a capital ship tonnage ratio of 5:5:3 (USN, RN, IJN) which mandated Japan maintain a smaller fleet, it effectively broke up the worrisome Anglo-Japanese alliance, but alternatively, by prohibiting fortification on its Pacific possessions, it essentially conceded regional naval dominance of the Western Pacific to the Imperial Japanese Navy.

Building up to treaty limits became the new goal of the post-Washington Treaty US Navy. With plenty of aircraft carrier tonnage to fill and unregulated quantities of other warships of less than 10,000 tons, the US Navy slowly began to pursue building programs in the 1920s that focused on these areas for potential growth. The Navy's first post-World War I building and modernization authorization came in 1924 and specified the modernization of existing coal-burning battleships and the conversion of the *Lexington* and *Saratoga* from cruiser hulls to aircraft carriers in accordance with the Washington Treaty. Additionally, eight cruisers were ordered laid down prior to 1927. However, even with this influx of modern cruisers, the US Navy remained understrength in modern cruisers relative to other major navies. A second cruiser bill designed to address these shortfalls was introduced, but died amid talk of a new disarmament conference in Geneva.

Geneva Conference

The Japanese naval building program of 1923, which included cruisers, destroyers, and submarines alarmed the other Washington Treaty signatories, and was seen as not in keeping with the spirit of the 1922 accord by both the British and US governments. As a result of this building program, the US Navy, through its advocates in Congress, began a program of cruiser construction in 1924 of five heavy cruisers (9,100 tons), and a further ten were requested in 1927.

It was against this backdrop of an unregulated cruiser arms race and the failure of the League of Nations-sponsored Preparatory Commission to achieve accord on the cruiser issue that the five powers agreed to meet on their own at Geneva in 1927. The US favored extending the 5:5:3 ratios to cruisers and setting the US limit at 400,000 tons. The French and Italians opted out of attending, but the Japanese and British, both anxious to avoid a cruiser arms race accepted the invitation. Britain's position mirrored the US', but increased the total tonnage to 500,000. By extending the ratio, this would allow the Japanese to build up to 325,000 tons of cruisers. This was unacceptable to the US Navy as they were positive that regardless of treaty maximum limits, they could only get Congress to fund 400,000 tons of US construction. If this came to pass, the British limits would gravely endanger the Navy's position in the Western Pacific and were therefore rejected. The conference was at an impasse and adjourned on 4 August 1927 without agreement.[40]

In response to the failed conference, in December 1927 President Coolidge pushed through Congress a building program that authorized the construction of one small carrier (*Ranger*) and fifteen heavy cruisers to be laid down over three years.[41] Japan and Britain, each alarmed by the US program, reacted by accelerating their own cruiser building programs.

London Naval Treaty

The political landscape surrounding naval disarmament changed yet again in 1929, when fellow pacifists Herbert Hoover and Ramsay MacDonald both rose to head their respective governments in the United States and Britain. The Great Depression induced widespread need for fiscal austerity throughout the world's governments and their respective navies. The leaders of the US, Great Britain, and Japan sought economic relief through a new round of negotiated multinational disarmament that enabled budget trimming without significantly impacting any one country's national interests. The London conference was convened among US, British, and Japanese delegates on 21 January 1930, and an accord was reached and signed three months later on 22 April 1930. As with the Washington Treaty, several refinements of important definitions emerged, among them, the elimination of armament restrictions for aircraft carriers signified that warship's emergence as a viable weapons platform whose potential utility in combat could no longer be judged by the number of guns mounted aboard.

Aircraft Carrier: (Change from Washington Treaty) any surface vessel, whatever its displacement designed for the specific and exclusive purpose of carrying aircraft and so constructed that aircraft can be launched therefrom and landed theron.

Cruisers: Surface vessels of war, other than capital ships or aircraft carriers, the standard displacement of which exceeds 1,850 tons, or with a gun above 5.1 inch. Cruisers were then subdivided into two categories, those with guns greater than 6.1 inch, and those with guns not above 6.1 inch.

Destroyers: Surface vessels of war the standard displacement of which does not exceed 1,850 tons and with a gun not above 5.1 inch.[42]

With all of the signatories having to scale back their naval building programs as a result of the economic impact of the Great Depression, these definitions allowed them to specify additional limits on warship construction to that already agreed on in the Washington Treaty ten years earlier. Clearly, part of the intent was to allow each signatory to focus on his own domestic economic recovery.

Under the increasing political and economic pressure to secure a treaty regardless of its potential negative strategic impact on the US Navy, Hoover's delegates reached an accord which effectively extended the conditions agreed to in the Washington Treaty to cruisers as well as an extension of the moratorium on capital ship building until 1937.[43] Specifically, from 1930 to 1936 the US was allowed to build fourteen heavy cruisers, but would have to delay laying down the final one until 1934. This effectively gave the Japanese a 10:10:7 cruiser ratio until the end of the building program. Submarine parity was established between the US, the UK, and Japan at 52,700 tons. The 10:10:7 ratio was also extended to destroyers, as their maximum allowable tonnage and armament was now defined by the same treaty. When the treaty was signed, destroyers made up only slightly more than 15 percent of the US Navy's total warship tonnage, and within five years the aging World War I era destroyers were due to be decommissioned, leaving only eight modern, front-line destroyers in service. Despite their concerns over destroyer force levels, the US Navy leadership did not see the treaty's limitation on destroyer tonnage as significant since it was believed that a fleet of destroyers could be constructed rapidly at the commencement of any conflict.[44] The London Treaty accomplished what it was intended to, in that it prevented a naval arms race by extending both the capital ship-building holiday and the systems of maximum allowable tonnage to other classes of warships. Table 2 summarizes the maximum allowable tonnage for cruisers, destroyers and submarines.[45]

Table 2. London Naval Armaments Limitation Treaty Maximum Allowable Tonnage Limits			
Categories	**United States**	**Great Britain**	**Japan**
Cruisers:			
(a) With guns of more than 6.1-inch (155-mm) caliber	180,000 tons	146,800 tons	108,400 tons
(b) With guns of 6.1-inch (155-mm) caliber or less	143,500 tons	192,200 tons	100,450 tons
Destroyers	150,000 tons	150,000 tons	105,500 tons
Submarines	52,700 tons	52,700 tons	52,700 tons

Looking Ahead

The year 1932 marks the end of the time frame for this introductory chapter. Events both abroad and domestically, make 1932 a natural end point for this scene-setting chapter. The Japanese invasion of Manchuria and establishment of a puppet government in 1931 posed a potential direct threat to US foreign policy interest with respect to its historic "Open Door" policy in China. Additionally, this expansion of Japanese influence in the region potentially threatened US influence and power throughout the region as well. As the US had effectively ceded regional power to Japan via the naval disarmament treaties, this demonstration by Japan of her intent to expand her sphere of influence through violence caused growing concern in both the US Navy and the government as a whole.

Meanwhile, 1932 also heralded the collapse of the German government and the rise of Adolf Hitler and his National Socialist government the following year. The new head of the German government had plans to reinvigorate Germany's sense of national pride and eventually reestablish its military prowess, despite restrictions in the Versailles Treaty. Germany's reemergence as a military power in the coming decade would directly challenge the interests of many of America's World War I allies. Germany's naval rearmament program included a potentially powerful U-boat arm designed to interdict commerce and potentially challenge US trade with Europe.

Finally, at home, November 1932 saw the election of Franklin D. Roosevelt, a politician with a long association with the US Navy dating back to his tenure as the Assistant Secretary of the Navy during World War I. His arrival in the White House set the stage for the US Navy's warship-building program to get back on its feet following four years without any appropriations.

Significant Causal Factor: 1919-1932

Without a doubt, the naval disarmament treaties of this period wielded the most influence over the warship-building programs from the end of World War I up until 1933. Their influence actually extended well past the mid-1930s. It was only brought to a conclusion when the treaty system collapsed and Japan withdrew from it, as will be discussed in a later chapter.

At the conclusion of World War I, the US Navy found itself with one of the most powerful fleets in the world. However, the US' inability to ratify the Versailles Treaty, and failure to join the League of Nations, coupled with its lone surviving economic potential to initiate an unmatchable naval building program, caused the US to be viewed as a potential threat by the now diminished naval powers of the world. This perceived international threat from the US was balanced domestically by the reemergence of strong isolationist and pacifist movements, which decried military spending and especially warship construction. This stature as the nation most economically capable of initiating a naval arms race along with its potentially unilateral foreign policy induced the world's naval powers to readily accept the US's invitation to the naval disarmament talks which led to the Washington Naval Treaty and the creation of a framework for guaranteeing international peace through naval disarmament.

The Washington Treaty's legacy in limiting capital ship construction forced the five powers to look to other ship types, particularly aircraft carriers and cruisers during the ten-year building holiday. In response to the Great Depression's imposition of severe austerity on national budgets, as well as fear of the unsettling effect on world order that a cruiser arms race could have induced, the London Naval Treaty was enacted with extended tonnage limits to this class as well as submarines. With the US Navy's fleet of aging World War I destroyers soon to fall well below treaty limits, building priorities following the treaty shifted again to fill these replacement requirements.

Therefore, as 1932 came to a close, US Navy warship-building programs had been well stifled over the previous decade, and although President-elect Roosevelt was coming to office, his economic policies seemed to indicate that he would be frugal with government spending, which did not bode well for a revival of warship building. However, changes in his economic philosophy and policies coupled with creative legislation and increased aggression by Japan soon created a set of circumstances where the US Navy would see its largest building program in many years

---

[1] Stephen W. Roskill, *Naval Policy Between the Wars* (New York, NY: Walker and Company. 1968).

[2] B. J. C. McKercher, ed., *Arms Limitations and Disarmament: Restraints on War, 1918-1939* (London: Praeger Publishing, 1992).

[3] U.S. Naval Arms Limitation Treaty, 6 February 1922, *Statues at Large* (1923-1925), vol. 43, pt 2.

[4] U.S. Naval Armament Limitation Treaty, 22 April 1930, *Statues at Large* (1929-1931), vol. 46, pt 2.

[5] U.S. Naval Armament Multilateral, 25 March 1936, *Statues at Large* (1935-1937), vol. 50, pt 2.

[6] U.S. Destroyers for Bases Agreement, 2 September 1940, *Statues at Large* (1939-1941), vol. 54, pt 2.

[7] U.S. Lend Lease Act, 11 March 1941, *Statues at Large* (1939-1941), vol. 55, pt 1.

[8] U.S. Naval Expansion Act, 14 June 1940, *Statues at Large* (1939-1941), vol. 54, pt 1.

[9] U.S. Naval Expansion Act, 19 July 1940, *Statues at Large* (1939-1941), vol. 54, pt 1.

[10] Edward S. Miller, *War Plan ORANGE* (Annapolis, MD: Naval Institute Press, 1991).

[11] Henry G. Gole, *The Road to Rainbow* (Annapolis, MD: Naval Institute Press, 2003).

[12] Edward J. Marolda ed., *FDR and the U.S. Navy* (New York, NY: St. Martin's Press, 1998).

[13] Robert Gardiner, *Conway's All the World's Fighting Ships 1922-1946* (London: Conway Maritime Press, 1980).

[14] "US Navy Active Ship Force Levels, 1917-Present" [database on-line], Washington DC: U.S. Naval Historical Center, accessed 24 September 2004; available from http://www.history.navy.mil/branches/org9-4.htm; Internet.

[15] Samuel Elliot Morison, *The Two-Ocean War: A Short History of the United States Navy in the Second World War* (Boston, MA: Little, Brown and Company, 1963).

[16] Robert W. Love Jr., *The History of the U. S. Navy,* vol. 1: *1775-1941* (Harrisonburg, PA: Stackpole Books, 1992).

[17] Kenneth S. Davis, *FDR, Into the Storm, 1937-1940* (New York, NY: Random House, 1993).

[18] William D. Leahy, *I Was There* (New York, NY: Whittlesey House Publishing Co., 1950).

[19] Henry H. Adams, *Witness to Power, The Life of Fleet Admiral William D. Leahy* (Annapolis, MD: Naval Institute Press, 1985).

[20] Elliot Roosevelt, ed., *F.D.R. His Personal Letters; 1928-1945,* vols. 1 and 2 (New York, NY: Duell, Sloan and Pearce, 1950).

[21] Robert Dallek, *Franklin D. Roosevelt and American Foreign Policy, 1932-1945* (New York, NY: Oxford University Press, 1979).

[22] V. R. Cardozier, *The Mobilization of the United Stated in World War II: How the Government, Military and Industry Prepared for War* (Jefferson, NC: McFarlane and Company Inc., 1995).

[23] William E. Leuchtenburg, *Franklin D. Roosevelt and the New Deal; 1932-1940* (New York, NY: Harper and Row Publishing Co., 1963).

[24] Alan Brinkley, *The End of Reform; New Deal Liberalism in Recession and War* (New York, NY: Alfred A. Knopf, 1995).

[25] Morison, 3.

[26] "US Navy Active Ship Force Levels, 1917-Present" [Database on-line]; Washington DC: U.S. Naval Historical Center, accessed 24 September 2004; available from http://www.history.navy.mil/branches/org9-4.htm; Internet.

[27] Love, 516.

[28] Ibid., 518.

[29] Roskill, 91.

[30] Ibid., 213.

[31] Love, 523.

[32] McKercher, 85.

[33] Ibid., 86.

[34] Ibid., 88.

[35] Ibid., 91

[36] U.S. Naval Arms Limitation Treaty, 6 February 1922, *Statues at Large* (1923-1925), vol. 43, pt 2.

[37] McKercher, 91.

[38] Love, 531.

[39] U.S. Naval Arms Limitation Treaty, 6 February 1922, *Statues at Large* (1923-1925), vol. 43, pt 2.

[40] McKercher, 178.

[41] Love, 556.

[42] U.S. Naval Armament Limitation Treaty, 22 April 1930, *Statues at Large* (1929-1931), vol. 46, pt 2.

[43] William M. McBride, "The unstable dynamics of a strategic technology: Disarmament, unemployment, and the interwar battleship," *Technology and Culture* 38, no. 2, (April 1997).

[44] Love, 561.

[45] U.S. Naval Armament Limitation Treaty, 22 April 1930, *Statues at Large* (1929-1931), vol. 46, pt 2.

CHAPTER 2

BUILDING A TREATY FLEET, 1933-1937

By the time of Franklin D. Roosevelt's inauguration in March of 1933 as the 32nd president, the US was languishing in the midst of the Great Depression. Beginning with the October 1929 US stock market crash, the Great Depression subsequently grew to an international credit crisis with the May 1931 failure of the Austrian Credit-Anstalt which led to massive international bankruptcies and over 12 million unemployed American workers by 1932. By the spring of 1933, after three hard years the nation's income had been cut in half, while over five thousand banks and nine million savings accounts were wiped out.[1] In this environment, the new president's immediate priority upon taking office was dealing with the domestic and economic issues affecting the nation. Warship building programs had to take a back seat to these domestic concerns, at least for the first year.

Despite his domestic priorities, the president's heart was never very far from naval matters. His life-long love of the Navy dated back to his receipt of a copy of Alfred Thayer Mahan's *The Influence of Seapower Upon History* as a childhood Christmas gift. Franklin D. Roosevelt followed in the footsteps of his distant cousin President Theodore Roosevelt when he also was appointed to serve as the Assistant Secretary of the Navy under Secretary Josephus Daniels during World War I in the Wilson administration.[2] He frequently demonstrated his continued affection for the Navy throughout his time in office by referring to the Navy as "us" or "we," while referring to the Army in less familiar terms.

Since the Navy had suffered in neglect under the Hoover administration, hopes were high that Franklin D. President Roosevelt would soon rectify the difficulties and infuse the service with the necessary funds to build it back up. Throughout the four years of the Hoover administration, not a single ship had been authorized. By 1933 the US Navy consisted of 372 ships (warships and other types) and displaced 1,038,660 tons, fully 150,000 tons below its allowable treaty limits. The real problem was that 288 of these ships were overage and increasingly in need of replacement. The Navy desperately needed to find a way to fund a robust warship-building program, but the current economic situation and the fiscal policies of the incumbent president made those efforts seem unlikely.

President Roosevelt was more credentialed as a military strategist from his time as Assistant Secretary than he was as an economist, but it was the needs of the failing national economy which were to demand his immediate attention as he assumed office. Despite the immediacy of the country's economic problems, President Roosevelt's affinity for the Navy never faded. He maintained a world view, similar to most naval officers of the day based primarily in the belief that American prosperity and security depended on access to raw materials available throughout the world's markets. President Roosevelt believed it was the Navy's responsibility to guarantee American prosperity and security. Further, the president believed that the principal challenge to American interests in terms of both commerce and security would come from Japan in the coming years; therefore, he expected the Navy to play a major role in dealing with this challenge.[3]

These beliefs were affirmed early in FDR's administration when in March of 1933, Japan officially withdrew from the League of Nations and disclosed the possibility of their abandonment of the naval limitations treaty that they had with Britain and the US. In April the US Ambassador to Japan, Joseph Grew, informed the new president that,

> Japan has probably the most complete, well-balanced, coordinated and therefore powerful fighting machine in the world today. . . . The Japanese fighting force considered the United States as their potential enemy . . . because they think the United States is standing in the path of their nation's natural expansion.[4]

In June, the president was informed by the Chairman of the House Naval Affairs Committee, Rep. Carl Vinson (D-GA) that the Japanese naval budget for 1933 reflected a 25 percent increase over the previous year's outlay, and in July the State Department informed the new president of the possibility of an impending Japanese attack on the USSR.[5] In short, the president had ample reasons to be concerned with Japan immediately upon entering office.

During his second cabinet meeting after taking office, the president learned of the existence of the Joint Planning Committee, which had been formed to plan for the possibility of war with Japan. War Plan Orange had its origins soon after the turn of the century when the US Navy and particularly those officers at the Naval War College recognized the growing economic and maritime threat of the Japanese empire and began a plan to counter its perceived threat to US power and influence in the region. US interests in the Western Pacific included its possessions in the Philippines, Guam, and, Hawaii, and its continued Open Door trade policy with China. By the early 1920s the plan's focus had shifted away from guaranteeing access to China and towards countering Japan. Through the 1920s and into the early 1930s the plan underwent many modifications and adjustments reflective of the personalities involved in the planning efforts, incorporation of new technologies, treaty limitations, and evolving strategy.

The plan, although frequently modified, consisted of three basic phases. In Phase I, Japan, code-named "Orange," would initiate the conflict by attacking to seize the lightly defended American, "Blue," outposts to assure its access to necessary raw materials in the south and west. The blue navy, concentrated in homeports along the west coast of the United States would then mobilize in the Eastern Pacific. In phase II, Blue's fleet would steam westward across the Central Pacific toward seizure of the Philippines. Orange would avoid decisive conflict, instead resisting with expendable forces in an effort to attrite Blue while trading distance for time. Blue would continue to advance and retake the Philippines and eventually the two battle fleets, in the finest Mahanian tradition, would meet for a decisive engagement, in which American dreadnoughts would prevail. In the final phase, Blue would surround and assault the Japanese home islands and win the war.

Previous to Versailles Treaty's directive for the handover of the Mandate Islands to Japan, the plan featured an aggressive thrust of the US Fleet across the Pacific toward the recapture of the Philippines. Japanese possession of these islands located astride the sea lanes of communication to both the Philippines and Guam spurred the 1921 modification to the plan to feature a more cautious, island-hopping campaign to defeat the Japanese.[6] The nonfortification clause of the Washington Treaty drove much of the planning effort of the 1920s as naval planners were forced to conceive ways in which to conduct an extended naval campaign without the benefit of an advanced base to support it. By 1923 the island-hopping aspects of the plan had been removed in favor of a return to the rapid naval thrust westward.[7] Figure 1 depicts the strategic location of the Mandate

Islands and illustrates their position astride US sea lines of communication to Guam, the Philippines, China, and the rest of the Western Pacific.

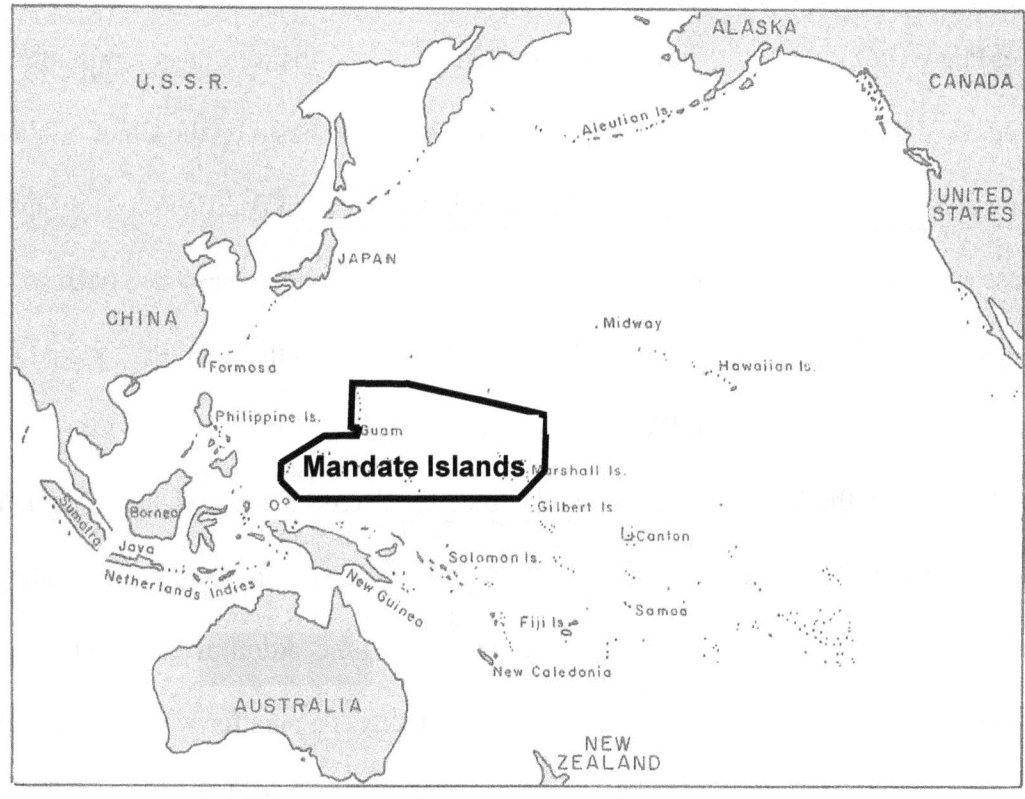

Figure 2.   Mandate Islands
Source: Martin Gilbert, *First World War Atlas* (NewYork, NY: The Macmillan Company, 1970), 145.

In the mid-1920s the rapid thrust of Blue capital ships from the West Coast of the United States to retake the Philippines played out with unfavorable attrition during naval war games and was modified to include several logistics stops in route. As President Roosevelt took office these logistics stops along the central thrust toward the recapture of the Philippines had been further modified into an island-hopping campaign through the Mandates themselves.[8]

Just prior to the election of the new administration, the latest War Plan Orange called for the phased departure of some 317 warships from Pearl Harbor with which to conduct Phase II of the plan.[9] At the time, less than 200 warships were in commission. By 1932, the Office of Naval Intelligence, in response to a proposal by the Chief of Naval Operations regarding increased US Navy presence in the Western Pacific as a deterrent to Japanese aggression in Manchuria, responded that they believed the Navy had been so weakened by economic neglect under the Hoover administration that it could not conduct an Orange scenario war.[10] Naval War College analysts judged that the US Navy's capacity to fight in the Western Pacific had declined to "decided inferiority" against their Japanese counterparts.[11] Given the capabilities gap between what the Orange plan called for and what the US Fleet was capable of executing at the time, Admiral J. O. Richards, later to command the US Fleet, called the Orange plan, "Less a plan for waging war than a plan to justifying a Navy."[12] Thus, on the eve of President Roosevelt's arrival, the Navy's leadership judged the fleet as ill equipped to carry out its principal war plan against its expected enemy. Much was required to remedy this situation, and the Navy hoped that the new administration would champion that effort.

The Process by Which Warships Are Built

Prior to an examination of the causal effects upon the annual warship-building programs of this phase, the process by which these programs were legislated and appropriated will be clarified in order to further illuminate the varied influences on the annual processes of building warships. The process began with the General Board making its recommendations to the Secretary. The General Board was a body of senior naval officers and other personnel and usually was comprised of the Chief of Naval Operations, the Commandant of the Marine Corps, and several other senior naval officers and distinguished civilians. Membership on the Board was at the invitation of the Secretary. As the members assisted the Secretary in analyzing strategic needs in order to forecast the service's building requirements, their sense of strategic priorities, technological innovation, tactical expertise, and national will needed to be in line with those of the Secretary. The General Board was responsible for interpreting the warship needs of the Navy and forwarding a recommended annual building program proposal to the Secretary of the Navy.

Approximately two years prior to the beginning of each fiscal year, which ran from 1 July of the previous year to 30 June of the fiscal year, the General Board would forward their recommendations to the Secretary of the Navy for new construction programs along with preliminary estimates of the costs associated. The Secretary then reviewed the proposal, sometimes modifying it with consultation with his military and civilian advisors, and then submitted it to the House and Senate Naval Affairs Committees. These committees would conduct hearings from which authorization bills emerged. The final step in the process was to have the House initiate an appropriations bill to fund the authorization, which would then be sent to the Senate and finally the president for final approval.[13]

It is important to note that under this system the US Navy's warship-building programs were funded individually on a yearly basis. As such, the scale and composition of these annual appropriations provide an excellent indicator as to the fleet's perceived needs of a given year. Additionally, the periodic nature of these appropriations also provides an excellent annual indicator as to the significant causal factors behind the building programs. As such, it is these annual appropriations, as well as their influences, that this chapter and following chapters examine beginning with the FY 1934 program as this was the first the new president signed.

Warship-Building Programs, 1933-1937

Roosevelt was very concerned about the reduced capability of the Navy and appointed Admiral William H. Standley as the new Chief of Naval Operations in July 1933. Admiral Standley, a former head of the Navy's War Plans Division, was intimately familiar with War Plan Orange and keenly aware of the fleets reduced capacity to execute the plan and therefore a strong advocate of building up the fleet.

The Navy did not receive the immediate bolster that some had hoped for with the arrival of a "Navy man" in the Oval Office. Rather than expand the meager FY 1934 building program, which he was presented, President Roosevelt approved it unaltered. In doing so, he authorized the construction of only four destroyers and one heavy cruiser.[14] Despite his love of the Navy, on this his first opportunity as president to benefit the Navy, economic and political realities forced him to act conservatively. The priority the new president placed on national defense relative to issues, such as economic recovery, was evident in his first federal budget in which he cut the military's budget by nearly one-third.

Further economic pressure was placed on the Navy in the form of a holdover from the Hoover administration. In an effort to balance the federal budget, a plan was enacted which divided the fleet into thirds and rotated each ship into a reserve status every third year as a means to drastically cut operating costs. Although opposed to such a plan, the Chief of Naval Operations (CNO) Admiral Pratt devised another plan that would save the government approximately $50 million of the Navy's $300 million budget. The plan that Pratt craftily devised to exclude aircraft carriers, battleships, and cruisers commenced in May 1933 and effectively reduced the operating capability of the Navy by one-third and sharply reduced shore activities. Fortunately for the Navy, a rapid congressional outcry effectively brought about the plan's demise, but the economic challenges of funding the fleet during the depression were all too evident in its intent.[15] Congress' reversal on this matter signaled a willingness to fund the current fleet, but their meager budget authorization for FY 1933 sent an unmistakable signal that regardless of an organic need to build, economic realities would restrict further funding unless increased political pressure was applied.

That political intervention came later in June 1933 in the form of Rep. Carl Vinson's creative application of funds from the National Industrial Recovery Act (NIRA). In as much as the cost of labor represented 85 percent of every dollar spent on naval construction, Rep. Vinson's addition of a naval construction provision to the act fit nicely into a bill conceived as a public works program aimed at increasing employment and consumer demand. These funds were used to fund two aircraft carriers, four light cruisers, twenty destroyers, and four submarines.[16] Notable in this mix of construction were the two carriers (*Yorktown* and *Enterprise*), each planned for 19,900 tons that would bring the US up to treaty limits for carriers.

Outwardly, President Roosevelt stressed that the naval aspects of the NIRA was focused on recovery rather than rearmament. His remark reflects a political reality of the country's general aversion to any program that could be seen as militaristic. Privately, however, he was very pleased to have had the opportunity to benefit the Navy. While discussing the NIRA passage with the Secretary of the Navy, Claude Swanson, he remarked, "Claude, we got away with murder that time."[17] This NIRA funding represented the largest shipbuilding appropriation since 1916 and soon drew the attention of Sen. W. E. Borah (R-ID), who spearheaded an amendment banning the use of future NIRA funds for military purposes, but by then, the Navy had its first building program of the new administration.

Meanwhile, in September 1933, the Imperial Japanese Navy (IJN) General Staff expanded its authority to conduct both peacetime and wartime planning by seizing this authority from the more moderate Navy Ministry. The IJN General Staff, long a detractor of the naval disarmament treaties that mandated Japan's fleet remain smaller and less prestigious than that of the US and Britain, soon began to purge the IJN of all officers closely associated with the 1930 London Treaty through forced retirements. Those note purged were marginalized within the IJN, and the drive for naval parity grew to dominate Japanese naval policy and planning.[18]

With the provisions of the Washington Naval Treaty set to expire on 31 December 1936, the looming negotiations to continue the naval disarmament framework were a prominent concern of the world's naval minds in 1934. President Roosevelt hoped to avoid a naval arms race by renewing and extending the provisions of the previous treaties at the coming second London Naval Conference and intended to persuade Japan to continue to accept less than parity with the US. Hoping to demonstrate outward resolve in advance of the coming conference he endorsed the 1934 Vinson-Trammell Act which authorized construction of 102 ships to bring the fleet up to its treaty limits by 1942.

Of note, Rep. Vinson failed to pass identical legislation in both 1930 and 1932 during the Hoover administration. The 1930 attempt failed due to the ongoing negotiations at London Naval Treaty, which might have reduced further the Washington limits, and thus rendered a building authorization irrelevant. The 1932 attempt failed because Congress was still committed to reducing federal expenditures as a means to combat the economic recession.

While President Roosevelt had gladly endorsed the fleet building programs, he worked hard at the same time to minimize the potential negative domestic perceptions of these programs. He was advised by Ambassador Norman Davis, who later served as head of the US negotiating team to the Second London Naval Treaty, that the naval programs caused a "great gloom . . . among a large section of our public."[19] The president sought to mitigate this public anxiety by explaining that although the Vinson-Trammel Act authorized the construction of 102 ships, it appropriated no funds for them, as that was the responsibility of future Congresses. He remarked, "It has been and will be the policy of the administration to favor continued limitation of naval armament. It is my personal hope that the Naval Conference to be held in 1935 will extend all existing limitations and agree to further reductions."[20] In this deft political maneuver, Roosevelt demonstrated he was able to skillfully appeal to the constituencies on both sides of the issue.

Following this massive authorization, the appropriations that funded to the FY 1935 building program were actually a lot less ambitious. It included the last four of the 8-inch gun heavy cruisers, three 6-inch gun light cruisers, fourteen destroyers, and six submarines.[21] Although the Secretary of State called immediately for a stronger fleet following passage of the bill, President Roosevelt had other priorities in mind when he approved the small appropriation for FY 1935. His primary concern was to pacify the liberal wing of the Democratic Party, which was reflexively against military spending. Similar to President Wilson's threat of a naval building program in 1921, President Roosevelt hoped to use the massive authorizations in the Vinson-Trammell Act to compel the Japanese to participate in the coming round of negotiations meant to extend the treaty system.[22]

Preliminary discussions in advance of the conference did not go well between the US, the UK, and Japan. Japan held fast to its desire for parity, while the US and Great Britain working together continued to insist on Japanese numerical inferiority, while also proposing an overall 20 percent reduction in tonnage among all parties. On 19 December 1934 the preliminary discussion ended without consensus. Ten days later the Japanese formally announced their required two-year notice of withdrawal from the Washington treaty. The timing of their announcement meant that their participation in both the Washington and London treaties would expire nearly simultaneously at the end of December 1936.

The breakdown of the preliminary talks caused President Roosevelt to push for a more aggressive building program in the hopes that it would lever the Japanese back to the negotiating table. President Roosevelt believed that the Japanese simply could not match the economic potential of the US and could not compete economically with the US in a naval arms race. He hoped that by announcing increasing building programs, he could ratchet up the pressure on Japan and force them back to the negotiating table. On

24 June 1935, he requested Congress increase its appropriation for naval construction in the 1935 Emergency Relief Act. This act provided funding for the robust FY 1936 building program, which included a carrier (*Wasp*), two light cruisers, fourteen destroyers, and six submarines.[23] Langley's conversion to a seaplane carrier made treaty limited tonnage available for *Wasp*.[24]

President Roosevelt was genuinely disappointed by his inability to get Japan to sign a new treaty. Not wishing to bear any blame for refusing to bend on the issue of US-Japanese naval parity, he instructed his negotiators to continue discussions with the remaining parties. Without a second London Naval Treaty, the US Navy's building programs would no longer be able to be sold to the public under the "build up to treaty limits" scheme. Roosevelt did not want naval building to appear to be in direct response to the Japanese building program.[25] His need to demonstrate success at the conference was further punctuated by the coming presidential election in late 1936.

In early January 1936, just days prior to the Japanese withdrawal, President Roosevelt attempted to coerce continued Japanese compliance at the London preliminary discussions through the announcement of his FY 1937 building program which included a nonthreatening array of twelve destroyers and six submarines.[26] Recognizing that this small building program would probably not compel Japanese compliance, President Roosevelt upped the stakes by including in the announcement his intention to commence a battleship replacement program should any of the signatories of the original Washington Naval Treaty commence their own replacement program. The program was meant as a final coercive device to convince the Japanese to rejoin the negotiations, but instead it had the opposite effect and hastened the sense of urgency in Tokyo to invigorate its own rearmament program to counter the American increases.[27]

Negotiations between the US, UK, and France eventually produced Roosevelt's desired agreement, which was signed on 25 March 1936 and was to remain in effect through the end of 1942. The new treaty preserved qualitative limits and provided for annual disclosure of building programs. The maximum tonnage for capital ships would remain at 35,000 tons, but with a reduced maximum gun caliber of 14 inches. Both of these restrictions were contingent on Japanese and Italian acquiesces by 1 April 1937. Carriers were limited to 23,000 tons and their armament was limited to 6.1 inches. Construction of cruisers in excess of 10,000 tons was prohibited. Furthermore, a prohibition on construction of ships between 8,000 and 17,500 tons was enacted. The most significant aspect of the treaty was the stipulation in Part IV, which provided for automatic tonnage increases in the event that nonessential parties exceeded the limits.[28] Table 4 summarizes the results of the Second London Treaty by illustrating the trigger or minimum tonnage-gun bore allowable in each category of warship.[29] Further, it illustrates that aside from heavy cruisers with guns in excess of 10 inches, or the placement of torpedoes on minor war vessels, all excesses of these limitations merely required notification of all other parties to the treaty.

Table 3

	Trigger Ton	Maximum Ton	Trigger Gun Bore Inch	Maximum Gun Bore Inch	Treaty Category Type	Prohibit Treaty Category Attribute
					Table 3. Second London Naval Treaty Categories	
Capital Ship	17,780	35,000	10	14	Notifiable	
Aircraft Carrier Decked		23,000		6.1	Notifiable	
Aircraft Carrier Undecked		23,000		6.1	Notifiable	
Heavy Cruiser	8,000	17,780	6.1	10	Prohibited	
Light Cruiser	3,000	8,000		6.1	Notifiable	
Scout	100	3,000		6.1	Notifiable	
Minor War Vessel	100	2,000		6.1	Unrestricted	Torpedoes
Submarine		2,000		5.1	Notifiable	

The inclusion of Part IV in the treaty afforded the US an escape clause for each limitation that the Japanese, not a participant, might choose to exceed. According to Captain Royal Ingersoll, USN, one of the treaty's drafters, "The treaty was written so that we could get out of every clause . . . if we found that Japan was in excess of the quantitative limits."[30] Therefore, the president received the political benefit of an arms limitation treaty prior to his election, while he ensured no real negative impact on the Navy, as the provisions were never fully enforceable.

President Roosevelt, alarmed over continued Japanese aggression in China, remained committed to reestablishing a Washington-style armament limitation framework. Although alarmed by the Japanese aggressive policy in China, especially their actions against the Chinese capital, Nanking. He admonished the Japanese, but was constrained in his response by his unwillingness to drive the Japanese away from a potential agreement over a renewed framework for naval arms limitation. However, when Japanese aircraft sank the US Navy's gunboat *Panay* on the Yangtze River on 11 December 1937, President Roosevelt abandoned hope that the Washington disarmament system could be reimposed on the Japanese.[31] This signified a fundamental shift in US policy towards Japan, which had a resounding impact on the US Navy and its annual building programs. The following year's building program, FY 1938, would reflect this change in policy.

With this event, the end of 1937 serves as a natural break in the narrative as it represents the end of President Roosevelt's belief that he could resurrect the treaty architecture among the great naval powers, specifically with Japan. Prior to the failure at the Second London Naval Conference, President Roosevelt truly believed that he could restore world order by extending previous accords and the potential introduction of a further 20 percent reduction in tonnage. When Japan left the conference, President Roosevelt's support for the resulting treaty was purely political as it held no real capacity to limit a naval arms race if Japan chose to commence one. This effective end of the treaty system marks the end of the first phase of analysis.

Causal Factors for Phase One (1933-1937)

There are several political influences on the US Navy's warship-building program during this phase of the analysis. The treaty system, as established in the Washington Treaty of 1922 and as modified in the London Treaty of 1930, served to regulate capital ships very effectively. The Second London Treaty was largely ineffectual as a regulatory device--as it was primarily a political instrument that President Roosevelt could display as evidence that he favored peace to an electorate who clearly wanted to hear that from their presidential candidate in 1936. As the US never did achieve its treaty-allowed warship levels during this phase, the most significant political causal factor of this phase is the pervasive pacifist and isolationist outlook of the American public, which was displayed by their elected representatives in Congress. Despite the authorization of the Vinson-Trammell Act of 1934, the Congress was unable to appropriate funds necessary to construct these massive increases in warships because the public simply would not have stood for their elected representatives voting for such a militant policy. President Roosevelt himself, when questioned about the act, had to justify it by saying that it did not actually fund any construction.

The most significant military causal factor of the phase from 1933 to 1937 was the need to modernize and enlarge the US Navy following over ten years of languishing under minuscule budgets. The four years previous to the first Roosevelt administration saw no funding for warship construction at all. The US seemed content during these years to allow its naval power to diminish, yet the Navy continued to plan for a potential Orange war, based mainly on the fleet it needed, instead of the fleet it had. As Japan continued its aggression against China, one of the ways the US might decide to counter them was via its fleet of warships. Although military requirements were real, they exhibit a diminished role in influencing construction during this first phase of analysis.

The most significant economic causal factor of this phase was the clear tie that lawmakers, particularly Representative Vinson and President Roosevelt had made between warship construction and economic stimulus. As discussed earlier, 85 percent of each dollar spent on building programs went directly into the labor force. The inclusion of appropriations to fund warship construction within the National Industrial Recovery Act signified a clear acknowledgement from a Congress that, under other circumstances, would not have approved such a bill.

Given the pacifist mood of America during this phase of the analysis and the seeming acceptance for diminished naval power, the economic forces represent the most significant causal factor of influence on warship construction. Were it not for the clear economic benefit, the limited building of this phase, such as it was, would not have been approved at all.

---

[1] William E. Leuchtenburg, *Franklin D. Roosevelt and the New Deal; 1932-1940* (New York, NY: Harper & Row Publishing Co. 1963), 18.

[2] Edward J. Marolda, ed., *FDR and the U.S. Navy* (New York, NY: St. Martin's Press, 1998), v.

[3] Ibid., 49.

[4] Robert Dallek, *Franklin D. Roosevelt and American Foreign Policy, 1932-1945* (New York, NY: Oxford University Press, 1979), 75.

[5] Ibid., 75.

[6] Edward S. Miller, *War Plan ORANGE* (Annapolis, MD: Naval Institute Press, 1991), 173.

[7] Ibid., 174

[8] Ibid., 173.

[9] Ibid., 147

[10] Robert W. Love Jr., *The History of the U. S. Navy,* vol. 1, *1775-1941* (Harrisonburg, PA: Stackpole Books, 1992), 582.

[11] Miller, 168.

[12] Marolda, 50.

[13] Stephen W. Roskill, *Naval Policy Between the Wars* (New York, NY: Walker and Company, 1968), 209.

[14] Robert Gardiner, *Conway's All the World's Fighting Ships 1922-1946* (London: Conway Maritime Press, 1980), 88.

[15] Love, 588.

[16] Gardiner, 88.

[17] B. J. C. McKercher, ed., *Arms Limitations and Disarmament: Restraints on War, 1918-1939 (*London: Praeger Publishing, 1992), 210.

[18] Ibid., 208.

[19] Dallek, 76.

[20] Ibid., 76.

[21] Gardiner, 88.

[22] Love, 593.

[23] Gardiner, 88.

[24] Ibid., 93.

[25] Dallek, 91.

[26] Gardiner, 88.

[27] Love, 594.

[28] McKercher, 221.

[29] U.S. Naval Armament Multilateral, 25 March 1936, *Statues at Large* (1937), vol. 50, pt 2.

[30] Love, 595.

[31] Ibid., 603.

CHAPTER 3

FLEET EXPANSION IN THE GATHERING STORM: 1938-1940

Whereas the expansion of the US Navy's warships from 1933 to 1937 was highlighted by a determined effort to build to treaty limits while simultaneously pursuing a continuation of the treaty system, the failure to secure Japanese acceptance of the Second London Treaty and loopholes in the subsequent treaty effectively signaled the end of the system which had formalized limitation on US warship construction since 1922. This chapter examines the impact that this end of the treaty system had on US warship construction from the end of 1937 through the fall of France.

As 1937 turned to 1938, the events in Asia and Europe began to show themselves as an increasing threat to world peace. Conflicts in Spain and China challenged the US's desire to remain neutral and threatened to plunge the world in another global war. As events unfolded from 1938 through to the fall of France in the summer of 1940, the political and economic influences, which had throttled the pace of construction, were gradually diminished, and the fleet's warship-building program began to produce a fleet of increasing combat capability. This chapter traces these shifts in causal factors behind the warship-building program from 1938 through the fall of France in the summer of 1940.

The attack on the USS *Panay* caused the US Navy to take stock of its capacity--or lack thereof--to deal with an openly hostile Japan. In one case, Rear Admiral George J. Meyer, commander of the 16th Naval District in the Philippines and one of the officers who would likely be among the first to bear the brunt of Japanese aggression, referred to the US Fleet as "woefully weak."[1] The 1935 revisions to War Plan Orange included an island-hopping campaign en route the Philippines, which would necessarily delay their liberation. To mitigate this delay in arrival of the US Fleet, Admiral Meyer suggested that a major naval base be constructed in the southern Philippines where warships of sufficient strength could be stationed to support US Army forces as the fleet advanced from their West Coast bases.[2]

In late 1937, Admiral Leahy endorsed a proposed revision to the Orange Plan which specified the Army ship two divisions of troops to the Philippines before war broke out or if that proved impossible, to place these divisions under the operational control of the Commander-in-Chief, US Fleet, to be used as an amphibious force against Truk, a Japanese fleet facility in the Caroline Islands. Unfortunately, the Army Chief of Staff, General Malin Craig, did not endorse this plan because the peacetime Army of 180,000 men did not possess the manpower to support it. Although they could not reach an accord on this particular revision, both agreed on the importance of defending the Alaska-Hawaii-Panama triangle. As a result of this shift of priority, the Army no longer felt that it should defend the Philippines while the Navy seized advanced bases in the Central Pacific. Although this impasse marked a temporary halt to joint planning against Japan, US Navy planning continued unilaterally and served to influence the General Board's warship-building recommendations to the Secretary of the Navy.[3]

With the treaty system in disarray and Japanese aggression now openly challenging the US, in the form of the USS *Panay* incident, the FY 1938 building program saw a noticeable increase over previous year's appropriations. Unlike the lean FY 1937 building program, which funded the construction of only eighteen warships, the FY 1938 program, which was approved by Congress on 21 January, was the largest in over ten years. It included funding for twenty-eight warships, including two light cruisers, sixteen destroyers, and eight submarines. Most significant, however, it also included funding for two new battleships of the North Carolina class, the first battleships the US had constructed since the Washington Treaty.[4]

One week after the FY 1938 building program was approved, Captain Royal Ingersoll returned from his mission to England, which failed to hammer out a bilateral Anglo-American blockade of Japan in response to the *Panay* incident. Ingersoll's failure was primarily due to two points of contention. First, the British were unwilling to dispatch their fleet to the Pacific when the crisis in Europe was worsening, and secondly, Ingersoll acknowledged that there were, "too few ships to make it effective."[5] Of note, however, Captain Ingersoll's mission produced one important success--he secured British agreement to allow the US to invoke the 1936 London Treaty escape clause, and thus enabled the US Navy to build and commission battleships in excess of 35,000 tons.[6] Following this agreement, the two North Carolina class battleships, approved in the FY 1938 building program and initially designed to carry twelve 14-inch guns, were armed with nine 16-inch guns to match Japanese weaponry being placed on its new battleships.

Upon hearing of the overall failure of the Ingersoll mission and on the advice from Admiral Leahy following the disagreement on a joint Army-Navy Orange Plan revision, President Roosevelt turned to Congress' perennial supporter of naval construction, Representative Vinson, for assistance in rectifying their shortfall of warships that was plaguing current diplomacy. The result was the Second Vinson-Trammel Act, which was passed on 17 May 1938 and authorized the president to exceed the construction limits of the 1934 Act by 20 percent. The Second Vinson-Trammel Act provided appropriation for two more South Dakota class battleships, two more 20,000-ton *Hornet* class carriers, nine light cruisers, twenty-three destroyers, and two submarines.[7]

President Roosevelt signaled a shift in his support of warship construction by openly lobbying for passage of the Second Vinson-Trammel Act. Whereas his public support for the initial act of 1934 was based on its economic benefits, by 1938 he was making statements as to the military necessity of the program. He believed that the diminished US Fleet was incapable of defending the nation on two oceans. He also maintained that the increases in construction were necessary to maintain desired warship ratios with Japan, whose ambitious construction program had begun in earnest in 1937. Rather than focusing on the "message" that the bill's passage would send to potential adversaries as he had in 1934, in 1938 President Roosevelt insisted that this building program would "keep any potential enemy many hundred miles away from our continental limits."[8] Ever the skilled politician, the president correctly anticipated the gradual swing of public sentiment away from isolationism and toward military preparedness for any eventuality given the increasingly hostile climate developing in both Europe and Asia.

Despite the growing indications of European turmoil, the FY 1939 building program was somewhat diminished in comparison to its predecessor. Although the US Navy had already begun to redistribute the already thinly stretched US Fleet in the Pacific by shifting assets to the newly established Atlantic Squadron, the FY 1939 program included funding for only five warships. However, these were all to be significantly powerful warships, as the program funded the construction of one carrier (*Hornet*), two new South Dakota class battleships, and two light cruisers.[9]

Meanwhile in September of 1938 at the Munich conference, Hitler exploited British Prime Minister Chamberlain's policy of appeasement by securing the transfer of the Sudetenland from Czechoslovakia to Germany. Although President Roosevelt initially hailed this as a diplomatic success, he harbored lingering suspicions of continued German expansion. Despite his acknowledgement of the fleet's inability to defend the US on two oceans, President Roosevelt began the process of splitting the US Fleet into what eventually became the Pacific and Atlantic Fleets by ordering the establishment of the Atlantic Squadron, consisting of two older battleships, seven heavy cruisers, and seven destroyers.[10] He further meant to demonstrate US resolve by ordering the 1939 fleet exercise, typically held annually in Hawaiian waters, to be held in the Caribbean.[11] Much as he had used the building programs of his first term as a means to project national will, President Roosevelt was now using fleet actions as a means to send signals to potential adversaries. The obvious intent was for a larger fleet to send a larger, less mistakable signal.

Admiral Leahy was also very concerned about increasing world tensions and ordered a complete overhaul of the Orange plan to reflect the changing political landscape. At this stage in its development, Plan Orange assumed unilateral US action against Japan who was presumed to be similarly acting alone. Captain Charles Cooke, the lead planner assigned to oversee the revision recommended that the Joint Board, responsible for joint Army-Navy war plans, to abandon the Orange plan in favor of five unique Rainbow plans, each of which assumed that either the US or its opponent was a member of a military alliance. Further recognition of troublesome events in Europe came in June 1938 when the carrier *Ranger*, four heavy cruisers, four destroyers, and two land-based patrol plane wings were transferred to the East Coast to join the Atlantic Squadron. As a deterrent to further Japanese aggression, Admiral Leahy and President Roosevelt also considered moving the remaining US Pacific Fleet to Hawaii, a move they deferred until later.[12]

Neutrality Acts

In 1935, with Japanese aggression in the Western Pacific, as well as the Italian incursion in Ethiopia threatening to boil over into larger wars, the Congress passed the first in a series of Neutrality Acts designed at limiting US involvement with belligerent nations. Initially passed as a temporary measure in 1935, the acts were signed into law in 1936. They contained among other things, provisions for a mandatory ban on arms trade and loans with belligerents, mandatory ban on arming US merchant ships trading with belligerents, but they allowed for a discretionary two-year period of cash-and-carry trade with belligerents if paid in cash and carried by foreign shipping. In 1939 the act was amended to restrict US shipping from a war zone around the British Isles.[13] In as much as these Neutrality Acts prevented direct support of belligerent nations, President Roosevelt tried diligently to diplomatically diffuse the coming storm in Europe. However, in the wake of Munich, congressional calls for increases in military spending became more commonplace as military construction was seen more through the lens of national and defense preparedness, rather than as a provocative gesture.

President Roosevelt scored a minor diplomatic victory against Japan and the constraints of the Neutrality Acts when he abrogated US participation in a 1911 trade agreement with Japan, which was set to expire in January 1940. Here again, this was primarily a political maneuver, which correctly read the public opinion swelling against Japan. Signaling his intention to deny Japan access to vital supplies previously provided by the US, the action went a long way to bolster Chinese morale, support Britain and other allies in the region, and demonstrated the president's ability to take meaningful international action despite restrictive policy of previous years.[14] His actions drew the concern of the US Ambassador to Japan Joseph Grew, who warned the president that increased economic pressure on Japan could lead Japan to strike south to seize the raw materials she required.[15]

Changes in the Navy Department

On 8 July 1939, Claude A. Swanson, President Roosevelt's only Secretary of the Navy since entering office in 1933, died of a heart attack. He had been plagued with near-continual illness since assuming his office. When speaking to former Secretary of the Navy Josephus Daniels during the Secretary Swanson's final months, President Roosevelt told his former boss that "Swanson is too sick a man to do much, but I haven't the heart to let him go," and also added, "You know I am my own Secretary of the Navy."[16] By the end of his term, Secretary Swanson had overseen a significant increase in warships in the fleet including new battleships with higher cruising speeds, 16-inch guns, and improved fire control equipment. Further warship additions included several dozen heavy and light cruisers, two new carriers with another on the way, over sixty new destroyers and thirty new submarines.[17] In personnel terms, the ranks had expanded by almost 1,000 officers and over 30,000 enlisted men. Although not yet fully capable of carrying out its wartime duties, the US Navy was vastly more prepared for war in 1939 than it had been when he entered office.

Charles Edison, the son of famous inventor Thomas A. Edison, was initially appointed as Assistant Secretary of the Navy in February 1936 to fill the tragically sudden vacancy when Henry L. Roosevelt, President Roosevelt's cousin died. Edison served ably as Assistant Secretary, frequently filling in for the ailing Swanson. Three years later, following the death of Secretary Swanson, Edison was elevated to be his replacement and officially assumed the office in January 1940. A man of considerable intellectual and business skills, he immediately increased oversight and management of navy yards, including construction schedules, contracts, and materials. In 1938, his duties were expanded by his appointment as Coordinator of Shipbuilding in order to better manage all the activities of all bureaus and agencies associated with that effort.[18]

In a 28 December 1938 memorandum to the Secretary, Assistant Secretary, and the CNO, President Roosevelt admonished the Navy's shipyards for their inefficiency in taking forty-two to forty-four months to construct the latest destroyers. He directed specific actions to increase productions schedules and closed by saying: "We are all of us being seriously criticized and it is time to get action."[19] In response to the president's frustration over delays in construction schedules, Assistant Secretary Edison established a system of inspections and reporting procedures by which the shipbuilding industry's fiscal and labor utilization was closely scrutinized. These business model standards of efficiency, established under then-Assistant Secretary Edison, would serve the Navy well in the years of increased warship production which were to follow and were instrumental in shifting the industry's peacetime perception of building programs as a means to guarantee work for the yards to one of real-readiness projects.[20]

Unfortunately for Edison, he had the misfortune of serving as secretary under a president who had himself served as an assistant secretary some twenty years previous. President Roosevelt effectively reduced traditional responsibilities of the Secretary by keeping for himself all decisions to do with naval strategy, war plans, promotion, and flag officer selection. Despite Edison's obvious competence, President Roosevelt refused to let someone else run the Navy without injecting himself in the process from time to time. In a 10 May 1939 memorandum to his naval aide, President Roosevelt, ever the ship designer and concerned about the growing threat from Germany's new pocket battleships, directed the CNO to determine whether two 8,000-ton light cruisers might successfully mount four 11-inch guns plus as many 5-inch dual purpose guns as possible. In his own disdain to current US cruiser firepower, he continued: "I still think an 8,000 ton light cruiser mounting on ten 6-inch guns, provides too light an armament for this tonnage."[21] Although the General Board deemed the president's proposal unfeasible, his "hobby" of ship design would become more pronounced as the US became more involved in the brewing war. President Roosevelt was also to play a role in the design of the destroyer escort, which was to play a large role as the war progressed, particularly in the Pacific.

Additionally, the president never shied away from the opportunity to push improvements on the new Secretary, especially when it came to economic efficiencies. In a 29 December 1939 memorandum to then-acting Secretary Edison, he wrote:

> My special ire has been raised of late by the design for non-combat ships. The Navy cost for such ships is exorbitant and, in my judgment, can be reduced at least 33% by the use of standard commercial construction. . . . It should be

remembered by the service that every dollar saved in the construction of non-combat ships means more dollars that can be spent for the construction of an additional number of combat ships. That thought should be posted in every office of the Department.[22]

Fortunately, Secretary Edison was uniquely skilled as a businessman to tackle the efficiency problem. He skillfully proposed and helped guide through Congress a bill that combined the bureaus of engineering and construction and repair into the Bureau of Ships. Additionally, he created the position of Under Secretary of the Navy, and charged the new office with coordinating procurement and materiel. As a testament to the production efficiencies achieved under this system, by early 1940, so many newly constructed warships were entering the fleet that President Roosevelt had to authorize the Naval Academy to graduate that year's class a semester early, so that the new ensigns could help alleviate the critical shortage of officers needed to man these ships.[23]

In this climate of growing military necessity and increasing political acceptance of military spending, the FY 1940 program included funding to construct two of the newly designed 33-knot, 45,000-ton Iowa posttreaty class battleships, two light cruisers, eight destroyers, and eight submarines. The FY 1940 appropriation reflected Edison's pursuit of construction efficiencies by focusing on efficient production of proven designs, rather than newer and potentially less-efficient classes of warships. Of the eight destroyers orders, all were off the earlier Gleaves class, and of the eight submarines, six were of the earlier Tambor class.[24] It was clear that he hoped to reduce production timelines by focusing on improved efficiencies captured in repetitive production of proven classes of warships. Included within the FY 1940 appropriation were funds designated to modernize five World War I era battleships and build a third set of locks for the Panama Canal, wide enough to accept the new Iowa class.[25] Despite these appropriations, by 1939, in almost every type of warship category, the Japanese had achieved parity with the US Navy or in some cases, had exceeded US capabilities.

Within one month of Secretary Swanson's death, Admiral Leahy's term as Chief of Naval Operations came to a close, and Admiral Harold R. Stark relieved him in August 1939. Admiral Leahy's retirement was brief as he transitioned to assume the duties as Governor of the island of Puerto Rico, before being reassigned to represent President Roosevelt as his ambassador to Vichy France. As a testament to his deep personal relationship with the president, he would later return to active duty as the president's Chief of Staff during the war years. This additional changeover of senior naval officials came just as Europe was bracing for war. German troops occupied Czechoslovakia in March, which only fed Hitler's appetite and led to his demand for the land surrounding the Polish port city of Danzig. Poland's refusal to accept Soviet troops on her soil as a guarantee against German aggression led Stalin to join with Hitler in the Nazi-Soviet nonaggression pact signed on 27 August 1939.[26]

On 5 September, in response to the declaration of rival blockades and war zones, President Roosevelt declared that the US was creating a Western Hemisphere Neutrality Zone off the East and Gulf Coasts of the United States, within which belligerent nations' warships would not be permitted to operate. Responsibility to maintain this zone was assigned to Admiral Johnson's fledgling Atlantic Squadron, only a year old at the time. Realizing that the Atlantic Squadron did not possess the ships necessary to effectively patrol the vast area of this zone, Stark successfully lobbied Congress for funds to recommission and modernize forty World War I era destroyers out of the Navy's escort reserve force.[27]

The FY 1941 building program, announced in early 1940 continued the steady building efforts of the previous years since Second London. It included funding for twenty-one warships including the first of the new Essex class aircraft carriers, two Iowa class battleships, two light cruisers, eight destroyers, and eight submarines.[28]

Stark, who was focused on events in Europe, felt that an Allied defeat might create a scenario, which the Japanese would seek to exploit in Asia. He believed that the lack of strength of the US Fleet in the Pacific made it "not now fully prepared"[29] for a Pacific war and wanted to avoid one until problems in Europe could be rectified. President Roosevelt, disappointed with the Navy's delay in establishing an effective antisubmarine patrol along the East and Gulf Coasts, as well as within the Caribbean, directed the Secretary of the Navy to rapidly establish these patrols, that their methods of search and track be clearly defined (he defined them), that contacts be tracked day and night, and that planes report all sightings immediately up their chains of command.[30] It was not until 6 December 1940 that all forty destroyers were either on station or en route to their patrol areas.[31]

In late 1939, following the fall of Poland, Admiral Stark sent a proposal to Congress which requested an additional 400,000 tons above the 1.5 million tons ceiling established in 1938. The bill sailed through the House, but the Senate was another matter. The Senate Naval Affairs Committee Chairman Sen. David Walsh, a staunch isolationist from Massachusetts, orchestrated the bill's stagnation and reduction until war resumed in Europe with the German attack into France. The bill, which is discussed in the following chapter, was reduced to only 167,000 tons by the time it finally passed.

The temporary cessation of German military aggression following their victory in Poland seemed to indicate a calming of Europe through the spring of 1940. Until the Germans recommenced their attacks in May 1940 with their assault on the Low Countries and France, Senator Walsh was able to allow the bill to languish in the Senate until it was finally passed on 14 June 1940.[32]

As the Germans advanced through France, the gravity of the situation in Europe in the eyes of the US Navy leadership was evident in the recommendation of the Navy's War Plans Division on 17 June 1940 to transfer the entire US Fleet, less one battleship division to the Atlantic Squadron. As expressed by Captain Cooke on 22 May, "The loss of the British fleet, or the loss of its effective use, points to the collapse of the British Empire with the consequent complete collapse of the world economic and political structure."[33]

The fall of France in June 1940 marks a natural end to this phase of the analysis. From 1937 until the fall of France, the US had appropriated funds to construct seventy-four warships, including two carriers and eight battleships. The fall of France would have an immediate impact on future building programs and will be discussed in the following chapter, which covers the final phase of the analysis. The US now viewed itself as the guarantor of British survival against expected continued Nazi assault. Prior to the fall of France, the US Navy's warship-building program had been largely focused on increasing capability to meet an increasing global threat. This temper of public opinion in reaction to this new development, as well as the reality of the immediacy and reality of the situation now facing Britain, enabled the US Navy's warship-building program to rapidly increase in the months to follow.

Causal Factors

The most significant military causal factor of this phase from the end of 1937 until the fall of France was the rise of maritime threats to the US's interest from both the Japanese in the Pacific and the Germans in the Atlantic. Japan's increasingly open dissatisfaction with the ratio-based treaty system in the early 1930s led to her withdrawal from the Second London Conference in 1936. Once free from the limits of the treaty system, Japan began a robust building program meant to eliminate their warship disparity with the US. As the US had maintained a fleet at lower than allowable limits, achieving parity with the US Navy did not necessarily mean building to the US's allowable treaty limit for warships. Meanwhile, Germany was in the process of rapidly rearming and had constructed a limited sized navy, which included relatively small numbers of potentially lethal warships, such as pocket battleships and submarines. Both Japanese building and German rearmament posed very-real military threats to the US and its allies. The problem was in getting the public and the Congress to recognize these threats, and thus enable to US Navy to build warships to counter them.

The most significant political causal factor of this phase of the analysis was the domestic isolationist and pacifist agendas, which held considerable sway within the Congress. Despite increased tensions across the globe and increases in the Japanese building program, domestic political will remained aligned against "provocative" military spending. President Roosevelt, himself a savvy politician, frequently put aside his affinity for the Navy to appease this significant block of public and congressional opinion throughout this phase. His ardent pursuit of a treaty at the Second London Conference, despite Japan's withdrawal, was indicative of this tendency of the president to play to the electorate. His desire to see the Navy enlarged to counter these growing threats would have to wait until an incident arose to galvanize public opinion in favor of construction. The fall of France and the Low Countries in the early summer of 1940 would provide that stimulus and served to have a dramatic impact on the building programs immediately thereafter.

Economics played a minimal role to influence warship construction during this phase. As in the early 1930s, funds for shipbuilding continued to provide large amounts of economic stimulus to the workforce, but as the "New Deal" was dying out from 1938 onward, the desire to use deficit-based defense spending as a tool to support factions of the labor force had largely faded. No longer would the economics of the New Deal provide the principal stimulus for warship construction as it had during the first phase of the analysis.

Overall, the most significant causal factor of this phase was the military influence of the Japanese increases in warship construction, as well as the rapid rearmament of Germany. The leadership within the US Navy increasingly recognized the growing threat to US interests in both hemispheres, but since the actions of each country were not perceived to have been egregious enough by US public opinion, neither swayed the predominant isolationist and pacifist outlook of the US public and Congress. Consequently, the US Navy was unable to increase its annual budgets for warship construction and saw them remain relatively constant in size despite the growing threats.

Despite this phase's relative moderate construction appropriations, significant combat capability was added to the US Navy during this period. Two carriers, eight battleships, eight light cruisers, along with thirty-two destroyers and twenty-four submarines were all funded in the annual programs of this phase. Had the international circumstances been severe enough, the military requirements, which drove these building programs, would have been easily increased to the levels seen following the fall of France. The US Navy had long identified its shortfalls in numbers of warships but had been unable to overcome the antibuilding influences of isolationism and pacifism, as well as the economical realities of federal appropriations budgets. The military requirements of the Navy were not being fully met by these building programs, but great care was taken to ensure what money was budgeted for building programs was spent wisely

---

[1]Robert W. Love Jr., *The History of the U. S. Navy,* vol. 1, *1775-1941* (Harrisonburg, PA: Stackpole Books, 1992), 606.

[2]Edward S. Miller, *War Plan ORANGE* (Annapolis, MD: Naval Institute Press, 1991), 255.

[3]Love, 607.

[4]Robert Gardiner, *Conway's All the World's Fighting Ships, 1922-1946* (London: Conway Maritime Press, 1980), 88.

[5]Love, 604.

[6]Ibid., 604.

[7]Ibid., 607.

[8]Ibid., 608.

[9]Gardiner, 88.

[10]Love, 611.

[11]Ibid., 611.

[12]Ibid., 610.

[13]Ibid., 618.

[14] Robert Dallek, *Franklin D. Roosevelt and American Foreign Policy, 1932-1945* (New York, NY: Oxford University Press, 1979), 195.

[15] Edward J. Marolda, ed., *FDR and the U.S. Navy* (New York, NY: St. Martin's Press, 1998), 54.

[16] Paolo E. Colletta, *American Secretaries of the Navy,* vol. 2 (Annapolis, MD: Naval Institute Press, 1980), 657.

[17] Marolda, 80.

[18] Colletta, 672.

[19] Elliot Roosevelt, ed., *F.D.R. His Personal Letters; 1928-1945,* vols. 1 and 2 (New York, NY: Duell, Sloan and Pearce, 1950), 843.

[20] Colletta, 670.

[21] Roosevelt, 881.

[22] Ibid., 978.

[23] Colletta, 672.

[24] Gardiner, 88.

[25] Love, 612.

[26] Ibid., 609.

[27] Ibid., 619.

[28] Gardiner, 89.

[29] Love, 612.

[30] Roosevelt, 937.

[31] Ibid., 963.

[32] Love, 620.

[33] Ibid., 621.

CHAPTER 4

THE SURGE IN BUILDING: A PRELUDE TO WAR, 1940-1941

This chapter examines the third phase of warship building. As the previous chapter ended, France was collapsing and England stood alone against the German aggressors. Whereas the US Navy's warship-building program had seen some revival as a result of the impending conflict and then outbreak of war in Europe, this chapter, the final phase of the analysis, covers a period when the inevitability of US involvement in the war grows by the day. As US public opinion is swayed towards the British cause, congressional opposition to building programs diminishes. Whereas prior to the fall of France, US public opinion tended to lean towards pacifism and isolationism, once the image of an aggressive Germany, a subjugated France, and a stalwart England were painted in the minds of the American public, the idea of coming to Britain's aid became more palatable and enabled their representatives in government greater freedom to enact appropriations to fund a larger fleet. This chapter examines the most immediate and substantial of the three phases in terms of numbers of warships appropriated. It explores the international and domestic situations that led to the appropriation of massive funds to build a fleet second to none.

In the summer of 1940, as the German Army overran country after country in Europe, isolationist sentiment began to crumble throughout America and within the US Congress. This sentiment has long been the underpinnings of resistance to increases in US warship construction. As it diminished, significant building programs were approved. Although the US population remained overwhelmingly opposed to entering the war as evidenced in opinion polls taken both before and after the outbreak of hostilities in Europe, resistance to national preparedness and to military aid abroad began to soften.

A series of Gallup polls taken during this period reflect public opinion. In February 1937, 95 percent of Americans canvassed said that America should not get involved in a war in Europe should it break out. An April 1939 Gallup poll, which asked whether the US should declare war if England and France went to war with Germany, resulted in 95 percent answering, "no." Even as late as September 1941, 87 percent of Americans polled did not think the US should declare war on Germany. Despite this sentiment, Americans acknowledged that the US would somehow be brought in to the conflict. The day before Germany invaded Poland, 60 percent responded, "yes" to a poll which asked, "If England and France should go to war with Germany do you think the US will be drawn into it?" This number rose to 85 percent as late as October 1941.[1]

The roots of this evolving sentiment were varied and complex. For years much of the press had argued that munitions manufacturers were the driving force behind American entrance into World War I, and some of the public still believed this to be true. So plausible was this theory, that it was the subject of Senate hearings in 1934.[2] Still others were less sentimental to England's plight and believed that she was more interested in preserving her empire than upholding the sovereignty of European democracies. Finally, there were still some residual bad feelings among Americans because Britain had failed to repay its wartime debts to the US made during World War I.[3] These isolationist sentiments gradually softened as international events unfolded in the remainder of 1940 and through 1941.

Germany's rapid success in its attack across the Lowlands and into France in May and June 1940 had a tremendous influence on US public opinion in favor of military preparedness. While France was still struggling with the attacking German forces, President Roosevelt both gauged and spurred this shift in public mood. He delivered a speech at the University of Virginia on 10 June, where he promised to mobilize the American armed forces while also providing military and naval aid to those nations who stood against the "Gods of force."[4]

The location and size of the US Fleet was in a state of flux in the summer of 1940. The previous March, the new US Fleet Commander Admiral James O. Richardson had taken the fleet to sea for its annual exercises with the intention of returning to San Diego in May. The Pacific-based US Fleet had been steadily drawn down to build up the fledgling Atlantic Squadron. Now, with events unfolding rapidly and unfavorably, the US Fleet was ordered to remain in Hawaii on 7 May as a deterrent against Japanese move to seize the raw material-rich Far East colonial possessions of either France or The Netherlands. Neither the diminishment of his fleet's combat power nor its relocation to Hawaii sat well with Admiral Richardson, who was a strident disciple of the Orange plan and resented the weakening and exposure to his striking force. More moves were on the horizon as the CNO Admiral Stark planned to move the entire US Fleet into the Atlantic if Britain were to surrender to Germany.[5] The new Rainbow 5 plan was crafted to deal with these significantly changed strategic issues and a reduced US Fleet in the Pacific. Rather than thrusting westward to relieve the Philippines, the plan only obligated the US Fleet to conduct a raid on the Marshall Islands within the first six months of the war's commencement. Admiral Stark felt that the Philippines would fall early in the war and that the Asiatic Fleet would be forced to retire from the Western Pacific.[6]

Expansion of the FY 1941 Building Program

The FY 1941 warship-building program had already been approved and announced in 1940 as per the normal legislative process. Initially, this program was made up of one aircraft carrier, two battleships, two light cruisers, eight destroyers, and eight submarines. Comprising only twenty-one warships, this program reflected the cautious optimism regarding the possibility of Germany halting its aggressions following its conquest of Poland. However, with the collapse of France, its meager numbers no longer reflected the strategic situation the US now found itself in. To meet the growing possibility of some form of US involvement in the conflict, in May of 1940, the FY 1941 program was dramatically increased by adding six more aircraft carriers, two battleships, four heavy cruisers, nine light cruisers, forty-five destroyers of three different classes, and twenty-eight submarines.[7] This huge program was the largest since World War I and represented a significant increase in US combat power once constructed.

Naval Expansion Act of 14 June 1940

With the FY 1941 building program already expanded dramatically, Congress, in anticipation of further warship requirements for a two-ocean war, passed the Naval Expansion Act of 14 June 1940, which President Roosevelt signed into law on the same day German forces occupied Paris. The act dramatically increased the US Navy's overall tonnage limits as defined in the Second Vinson Trammel Act of 1938 by a total of 167,000 tons, and further broke this down into specific warship classes as follows:

(a) Aircraft carriers, seventy-nine thousand five hundred tons, making a total authorized under-age tonnage of two hundred and fifty-four thousand five hundred tons.

(b) Cruisers, sixty-six thousand five hundred tons, making a total authorized under-age tonnage of four hundred and seventy-nine thousand and twenty-four tons.

(c) Submarines, twenty-one thousand tons, making a total authorized under-age tonnage of one hundred and two thousand nine hundred and fifty-six tons: Provided, That the foregoing total tonnage for aircraft carriers, cruisers, and submarines may be varied by thirty-three thousand four hundred tons in the aggregate so long as the sum of the total tonnages of these classes as authorized herein is not exceeded: Provided further, That the terms used in this or any other Act to describe vessels of designated classes shall not be understood as limited or controlled by definitions contained in any treaty which is not now in force.[8]

The Act also appropriated funding of an infrastructure necessary to facilitate the authorized growth in warship construction. It provided the president up to $35,000,000 to be spent on, "shipbuilding ways, shipbuilding docks and essential equipment and facilities at naval establishments for building or equipping any ship," and appropriated a further $6,000,000 for the production of armor or armament which, "may be leased, sold, or otherwise disposed of, in the discretion of the Secretary of the Navy, when no longer required for use under naval contract."[9]

New Man at the Helm: Secretary Frank Knox

President Roosevelt availed himself of the opportunity that events in Europe presented by retooling his cabinet as well and specifically the Secretary of the Navy. Knowing he would face continued resistance from entrenched isolationists and Republicans in the coming 1940 election, he sought to neutralize both these forces in nominating Frank Knox to relieve Secretary Edison whom he never favored. Although a well-known Republican and an adversary of President Roosevelt on economic recovery issues, Frank Knox was a staunch supporter of the president on matters of foreign policy.

He had a storied rise to power, which began during the Spanish-American War when he fought in Cuba as a member of Theodore Roosevelt's Rough Riders. Although he was forty-three when World War I broke out, he managed to secure himself a commission in the Army and served in France in command of an ammunition train where he rose to the rank of major.[10] Following his wartime service, he worked in the newspaper industry, rising to purchase the *Chicago Daily News* in 1931, where he achieved to national fame for his strident attacks on President Roosevelt's New Deal economic policy in his editorial columns throughout the 1930s. He served as the Republican Party's vice-presidential nominee for the 1936 election, but when Roosevelt won in a landslide, he returned to his newspaper business.[11]

Although Knox consistently opposed to the president's economic policies, he was an ardent supporter of the president's foreign policies throughout this period. When war broke out in Europe in 1939, Knox penned a front-page editorial that called for universal support of President Roosevelt's leadership in foreign affairs, the repeal of the Neutrality Acts, and a bipartisan cabinet.[12] President Roosevelt made room for Knox as the Secretary of the Navy by pulling strings within the Democratic Party to enable Secretary Edison to run for the governorship of New Jersey.

President Roosevelt knew that he had to lift the restrictions of the Neutrality Acts in order to free up his foreign policy and was advised by Knox that he might achieve this goal with the Congress if he included some Republicans in his cabinet. In early 1940, late in his second term, President Roosevelt took him at his word and nominated Frank Knox as Secretary of the Navy, along with fellow Republican, former Secretary of State Henry L. Stimson as Secretary of the Army. President Roosevelt's appointment of Knox was shrewd on several levels. With his new secretary, the president now had an ardent supporter of increased US involvement in support of France and Great Britain against Germany. Additionally, in Frank Knox, he gained a skilled communicator who knew how the publishing industry worked and was clearly capable of manipulating it for the administration's benefit. Finally, FDR hoped the inclusion of Republicans into the cabinet would convince those in Congress of the temperance of the administration and result in the lifting of the Neutrality Acts that limited US involvement in the conflict.

Knowing that he was being considered for nomination, Mr. Knox continued to use his editorial pulpit to support the president. In a front-page editorial in May 1940, he declared, "The German invasion of Holland strikes the hour of decision for the United States." He went on to call for new defense spending to include the construction of "the most powerful fleet in the world, as soon as humanly possible."[13] When his nomination was announced in June 1940, Mr. Knox, in a prelude to his coming skillful utilization of the media to the benefit of the Navy's coming surge in warship building, released the following statement: "National defense is not a partisan question. We are in danger now because we are inadequately prepared. The president has said that I can help him. If I can help him prepare for any emergency I must do so."[14] Shortly after the fall of France, Secretary Knox was confirmed on 11 July 1940.

Secretary Knox played a critical role in the warship-building programs in the final moments prior to US involvement in the war. His influence began prior to his assumption of office when he used his editorial pen to vigorously back the programs of the late 1930s and early 1940s. His influential opinion helped to sway countless readers and played a roll in the overall shift in American support of military spending in these critical years. Once in office, his skills as a businessman, leader, and savvy manipulator of the press would further benefit the Navy's building effort.

Naval Expansion Act of 19 July 1940

On 17 June, the same day that France asked Germany for an armistice, the CNO, Admiral Stark, anxious to maximize naval benefit from an advantageous shift in public and presidential mood, drafted an expansive shipbuilding program aimed at the creation of two separate and balanced fleets, one based in the Pacific responsible for executing some form of the evolving Orange plan, and one in the Atlantic responsible for operations in Europe.[15] Stark's proposed plan increased the fleet size by 70 percent, was projected to cost $4 billion, and would take eight full years to complete construction. Rear Admiral Ernest J. King, as one of the leading members of the General Board, raced the plan through the board's approval process overnight, so that it could immediately be brought to the Secretary's office for referral to Congress. The bill, which became known as the "Two Ocean Navy Act," was passed into law on 19 July 1940, only eight days after Secretary Knox assumed his office. Specifically, the act authorized a further increase in addition to the previous month's act of 1,325,000 ton in the following categories:

   (a) Capital ships, three hundred and eighty-five thousand tons;

   (b) Aircraft carriers, two hundred thousand tons;

   (c) Cruisers, four hundred and twenty thousand tons;

   (d) Destroyers, two hundred and fifty thousand tons;

(e) Submarines, seventy thousand tons: *Provided,* That each of the foregoing increases in tonnages for capital ships, aircraft carriers, cruisers, destroyers, and submarines may be varied upward or downward in the amount of 30 per centum of the total increased tonnage authorized herein so long as the sum of the total increases in tonnages of these classes as authorized herein is not exceeded.[16]

Funding ceilings were specified in section three of the act, which authorized shipbuilding expenditures up to $150,000,000, to ordnance and munitions production up to $65,000,000, and to armor production of up to $35,000,000. Additionally, in recognition to the looming threat of war and the need to cease reductions of fleet strength through decommissioning, sale, or lease, section seven of the act specified that, "No vessel, ship, or boat (except ships' boats) now in the United States Navy or being built or hereafter built therefore shall be disposed of by sale or otherwise, or be chartered or scrapped, except as now provided by law."[17]

Further Increases in the FY 1941 Building Program

Following its expansion in May, the FY 1941 building program was increased from its original size of 21 to 115 warships. Already a huge-building appropriation by previous standards, the FY 1941 program was radically enlarged again in late July following the Expansion Act's passage that same month, by a further 228 warships. These included: 4 aircraft carriers, 5 battleships, 6 heavy cruisers, 25 light cruisers, 151 Destroyers, and 37 submarines.[18] Taken as a whole, the initial FY 1941 building program along with its two additions now amounted to 343 warships. Considering length of construction and training time necessary before these new ships could join the operational fleet, the FY 1941 program constituted the bulk of the US Navy's Pacific fleet that fought World War II.[19]

Retooling the Department of the Navy

Upon assuming his position as Secretary in July 1940, Knox had only seven naval officers and seven civilians manning the Office of the Secretary of the Navy. Correctly anticipating the surge in construction and the magnitude of the overall effort, Knox set about immediately expanding and streamlining the functions of the office. He created the position of Under Secretary of the Navy, responsible for liaison with industrial agencies and supervision of contracts, and named New York investment banker James Forrestal to the post.[20] By 1941, he had expanded the office to include nine naval officers and twenty-five civilian employees. Additionally, Knox strengthened his staff's capabilities in two of the most critical areas of ship construction and public relations by hiring Joseph Powell and Frank Mason as special assistants, both of whom agreed to work for only one dollar a year in salary. Joseph Powell had risen to become one of the US's leading shipbuilders and served as the Secretary's personal technical advisor on naval construction matters. Frank Mason was hired away from his position as Vice President of NBC to help the Secretary organize the radio activities of the Navy's expanding public relations program.[21]

As a former journalist with forty-two years in the business, Secretary Knox was keenly aware of the potential power that the press could wield in helping sway public opinion in favor of the administration and the Navy. He knew that without assistance from a skillful public affairs campaign, the expanding naval construction program would meet resistance from the isolationists within Congress. As a means of emphasizing the increased importance of public relations, Secretary Knox announced in April 1941 the split of the Public Relations branch from Naval Intelligence into its own separate community and elevated the rank of its commander to Rear Admiral.[22] Correctly recognizing the influence of the press on public opinion and then by extension, the influence of the public on its elected officials in the Congress, Secretary Knox remained vigorously engaged in public relations throughout his tenure. He conducted weekly press conferences, published many articles in newspapers and periodicals, and delivered an average of two speeches a month directed at getting the Navy's message out to the public.

Despite Knox's efforts to the contrary, the Secretary's message was not always well received. Isolationists within the Congress were still a significant political force. In a 30 June 1940 speech to a governor's conference, Knox stated, "The time to use our Navy to clear the Atlantic of the German menace is at hand."[23] Senator Burton K. Wheeler responded that the Secretary should be, "thrown out of office,"[24] and Representative Hamilton Fish suggested that he be impeached for his hawkish views. However, the Chief Justice of the Supreme Court, Felix Frankfurter, wrote to Knox and informed him that, "When you're impeached can I leave the bench and become one of your counsel?"[25]

Destroyers for Bases Agreement, 2 September 1940

Britain had shaped its prewar planning for convoy escort operation in the Atlantic on the assumption that French escort vessels would contribute to the effort. In 1940, France possessed sixty-six destroyers of various classes.[26] British prewar building programs had focused on other classes of warships given France's excellent capability in escort vessels. When France fell, these escort vessels were no longer available to the Battle of the Atlantic. Additionally, the French fleet was now in the hands of the Vichy government, whose ability to prevent its falling into the hands of the Nazis was suspect. This unanticipated loss of escort vessels for the Atlantic campaign dramatically highlighted further accentuating her shortage in that area, additionally the image of Germany assuming control of the former French fleet and joining that with their own and their Italian ally's fleet was a very real threat to the Royal Navy itself. President Roosevelt sent his able and trusted advisor, former CNO, retired Admiral Leahy, to be the American Ambassador to the new Vichy government with guidance to prevent the turnover of the French fleet. In his letter of instruction to Admiral Leahy upon taking the position, President Roosevelt wrote:

> I believe that the maintenance of the French fleet free of German control is not only of prime importance to the defense of this hemisphere but is also vital to the preservation of the French Empire and the eventual restoration of French independence and autonomy.
> Accordingly, from the moment we were confronted with the imminent collapse of French resistance it has been a cardinal principle of this administration to assure that the French fleet did not fall into German hands and was not used in the furtherance of German aims. I immediately informed the French Government, therefore that should that Government permit the French fleet to b e surrendered to Germany the French Government would permanently lose the friendship and good will of the Government of the United States.[27]

President Roosevelt dearly wanted to provide support to the British government in the form of warships, but was restrained by the Neutrality Acts and a lingering isolationist mood in Congress. As early as 22 July 1940, in a letter to Secretary Knox the president stated that he feared, "Congress is in no mood at the present time to allow any form of sale."[28] Later in consideration of the restrictive Neutrality Acts, he instructed the Secretary, "You might, however, think over the possibility at a little later date of trying to get congressional action to allow the sale of these destroyers to Canada on condition that they be used solely in American Hemisphere defense, i.e., from Greenland to British Guiana including Bermuda and the West Indies."[29]

Meanwhile, Secretary Knox's public and energetic support of President Roosevelt's foreign policy did not go unnoticed by the British government. On the evening of 1 August 1940, Secretary Knox's dinner was interrupted by a telephone call from the British ambassador, who invited him to come to the embassy to discuss a matter of great importance to the British. The ambassador, Lord Lothian, repeated an appeal made twelve weeks earlier by Prime Minister Churchill to President Roosevelt, in which he requested the transfer of fifty overage destroyers to the Royal Navy. Politics and legal issues had prevented the earlier transfer, but much had changed both internationally and domestically since the initial request. Recent British losses in the Battle of the Atlantic in both destroyers and merchant shipping made the need for these fifty warships critical to British survival. Lord Lothian knew that Knox was especially sympathetic to the British struggle, and requested that he, "exhaust every means that he could before giving him a negative reply."[30]

Secretary Knox suggested that the deal might be acceptable if the US were to gain new bases along the East Coast of Canada and in British possessions in the Caribbean. The British government rapidly approved a plan, which included the sale of base sites for the destroyers. In order to comply with the Pan-American Treaty, however, the US was forced to reject the sale in favor of leases for the bases. Eager to assist Britain but unwilling to risk his upcoming election on the issue, President Roosevelt demonstrated just how precarious such an arrangement could be to his political viability when he first secured assurances from his Republican rival, Governor Wendell Wilkie of Kansas, in the coming presidential election that if he were to proceed with the deal, it would not be used as a campaign issue. In order to secure this assurance, President Roosevelt relied on

Secretary Knox to contact an old newspaper editor friend in Kansas and use him to approach the Republican nominee securely.

Despite these bipartisan arrangements, party politics still had a role to play in potentially spoiling the arrangement. As these fifty destroyers were originally slated for recommissioning into the US Navy, Senator Walsh, the powerful Republican chairman of the Senate Naval Affairs Committee, introduced an amendment in the 1940 National Defense Act which prohibited the overseas transfer of any American ships, munitions, or other war materials unless either the CNO or the Army Chief of Staff attested that the material to be transferred was not essential to the defense of the US. Awkwardly for Admiral Stark, this put him in the position to countermand presidential policy with regard to foreign transfers. In a 22 August letter to Senator Walsh, President Roosevelt attempted to convince the chairman of the overall benefit of the exchange to the US by saying,

> The fifty destroyers are the same type of ship which we have been from time to time striking from the naval list and selling for scrap for, I think, $4,000 or $5,000 per destroyer. On that basis, the cost of the right to at least seven naval and air bases is an extremely low one from the point of view of the United States Government--i.e., about $250,000![31]

The US Attorney General relieved Stark of his burden by providing him with a legal opinion that the bases constituted a greater value to US defense than the old warships, and thus allowed him to endorse his president's policies without causing incident.

Secretary of State Cordell Hull signed and made public the final text of the deal on 2 September 1940. The notable details of the agreement as quoted from its text are included below:

> His Majesty's Government will secure the grant to the Government of the United States, freely and without consideration, of the lease for immediate

Establishment and use of naval and air bases and facilities for entrance thereto and the operation and protection thereof, on the Avalon Peninsula and on the southern coast of Newfoundland, and on the east coast and on the Great Bay of Bermuda. . . . His Majesty's Government will make available to the United States for immediate establishment and use naval and air bases and facilities for entrance thereto and the operation and protection thereof, on the eastern side of the Bahamas, the southern coast of Jamaica, the western coast of St. Lucia, the west coast of Trinidad in the Gulf of Paria, in the island of Antigua and in British Guiana within fifty miles of Georgetown. All the bases and facilities …will be leased to the United States for a period of ninety- nine years. . . . In consideration of the declarations above quoted, the Government of the United States will immediately transfer to His Majesty's Government fifty United States Navy' destroyers generally referred to as the twelve hundred-ton type.[32]

Changes within the Navy

As Secretary Knox was increasing the effectiveness of the Office of the Secretary, disharmony continued to brew in the leadership of the US Fleet. Admiral Richardson continued to vehemently disagree with the weakening and repositioning of the US Fleet, and was actually the subject of an unsuccessful attempt by Secretary Edison to have him relieved in the final days of Edison's tenure in office. Admiral Richardson was finally ordered to Washington to explain his position in person to the president, the Secretary, and the CNO. The combined influence of these three along with Admiral Leahy did not cause him to alter his position. His refusal to alter his perspective, despite his superiors' unanimous dissent, earned him the angst of the assembled naval leadership, and resulted in his being relieved.

In February 1941 Admiral Husband E. Kimmel was named to command the Pacific Fleet. On the same day, the Atlantic Squadron was officially redesignated the Atlantic Fleet and Admiral Ernest J. King was appointed as its commander. Admiral King was ordered to end the neutrality patrols and prepare to escort American transatlantic shipping by 1 April 1941. As demonstrated by the fleet's move from San

Diego to Pearl Harbor, as well as by the creation of the Atlantic Fleet, US foreign policy and naval strategy had now become indistinguishably linked.[33]

Although the individual foreign policies of Japan, Germany, and Italy seemed to lack commonality, they all shared a potential common enemy in the US. Their unity in keeping the US out of the war was the instrument that brought them together on 27 September 1940 to sign the Tripartite Agreement, which marked the advent of the Axis Powers as an alliance. The agreement was designed to compel the US to remain neutral by guaranteeing that the other parties would declare war on the US if any one of them was attacked by the US. The implications of this agreement on the US Navy meant that it could no longer expect its efforts in the coming war to be solely in either the Atlantic or the Pacific. A two-ocean conflict for the US Navy, if war was indeed to come, now seemed inevitable.[34] Fortunately for the US Navy, this eventuality had been largely foreseen in the massive building appropriations of FY 1941.

Europe First

Once President Roosevelt had been reelected in 1940, Admiral Stark began to bring some coherence to the seemingly contradictory national policies of US rearmament and overseas military assistance, particularly to Britain. In a white paper that later came to be known as Plan Dog, Admiral Stark maintained that the survival of the British Empire along with increased US strength in its home waters is fundamentally in the US national interest. In clarifying the importance to the US of Britain's struggle with Germany, he maintained that, "If Britain wins decisively, we could win everywhere, but . . . if she loses . . . while we might not lose everywhere, we might possibly not win anywhere."[35] Therefore, he proposed that priority effort in a two-front war should be given to the European theater over the Asian theater. On 16 December 1940, Stark, upon the advice of Captain Alan Kirk, the US Naval Attaché in London, assessed that Britain was within six months of collapse if the current rate of shipping losses continued uninterrupted. The following month, President Roosevelt announced that the Navy would stand on the defensive in the Pacific, would not reinforce its forward-deployed Asiatic Fleet in the Philippines, and would make all preparations to convoy transatlantic merchant shipping to Britain.

Despite the previous transfer of destroyers to Great Britain, the Royal Navy's far-spread commitments coupled with losses at sea meant she still needed more escorts. Despite this need, Admiral Stark believed Britain also lacked the manpower to immediately man any further transfers of US warships. Therefore, he saw no alternative but to have the Atlantic Fleet prepare itself to prevent a German naval breakout and to begin escorting British convoys later in the year. On 2 April, he moved to bolster the Atlantic Fleet's strength to match its growing mission through the transfer of the carrier *Yorktown*, the battleships *Idaho*, *New Mexico*, and *Mississippi*, four cruisers, and two destroyer divisions from the Pacific Fleet to the Atlantic.[36] In demonstration of his view on US involvement in the war, the following day he told Admiral Kimmell, "The question as to our entry into the war, now seems to be 'when' and not 'whether'."[37] Stark also informed Kimmell to expect further transfers in support of the Atlantic Fleet's convoy escort mission as the CNO viewed the Atlantic Fleet as possessing a "force utterly inadequate to do it on any efficient scale."[38] By the late spring of 1941 fully one-quarter of the US Fleet had been transferred from the Pacific to the Atlantic.

Stark became more wedded to a defensive strategy in the Pacific. He went so far as to persuade the Joint Board to veto the American-British-Dutch Agreement, negotiated by Asiatic Fleet Commander Admiral Thomas C. Hart, which mandated the reinforcement of the Philippines with submarines and airpower. Given his limited resources, he was forced to assess the requirements of the Atlantic Fleet and the Lend Lease program as greater than those of either Pacific or Asiatic Fleets. Although much building had been appropriated by this time, particularly the FY 1941 program, which would provide for strong fleets in both oceans once constructed, the overall weakness of the US Navy forced the CNO to ration his forces between the Atlantic and the Pacific. His weakening of the Pacific Fleet to bolster the Atlantic surely sent signals to the Japanese, which emboldened them to believe themselves now capable of dealing with the weaker Pacific Fleet. Operating with a fleet incapable of accomplishing wartime missions in both oceans was about to play a role in bringing about US entry into the war and in the unexpected theater--the Pacific.

Lend Lease Act, 11 March 1941

In early 1941 Britain's situation in standing alone against Germany had become extremely precarious. President Roosevelt dearly wanted to assist but was unwilling and unable to commit forces in such a way as might directly drag the US into the conflict. The solution to this dilemma came in the form of the Lend Lease Act. Under this legislation, the US would produce and provide the war materials which Britain desperately needed, but on a cash-and-carry basis. According to the final draft of the Act,

> Notwithstanding the provisions of any other law, the president may, from time to time, when he deems it in the interest of national defense, authorize the Secretary of War, the Secretary of the Navy, or the head of any other department

or agency of the Government . . . [t]o sell, transfer title to, exchange, lease, lend, or otherwise dispose of, to any such government any defense article. Nothing in this Act shall be construed to authorize or to permit the authorization of convoying vessels by naval vessels of the United States. . . . Nothing in this Act shall be construed to authorize or to permit the authorization of the entry of any American vessel into a combat area in violation of section 3 of the neutrality Act of 1939.[39]

As approval of the bill required congressional approval, it spawned one of the final great debates on isolationism versus US support of an ally in need. Interestingly, the key factor in its approval was its acknowledged benefit to the US economy. Since 1940, the US economy had made a significant upturn, not because of the effects of New Deal policies, but primarily due to munitions production orders from Britain along with domestic consumption of wartime materials from the War and Navy Departments themselves.[40] Lend Lease was initially approved for Britain alone, but was later extended to include the Soviet Union as well.

FY 1942 Building Program

The massive FY 1941 program fulfilled most of the Navy's immediate needs to fight and win a two-ocean war. As a result of the largely fulfilled requirements and the full capacity of the nation's shipyards, the FY19 42 warship-building program was comprised of eighty-seven warships, huge by previous standards, but considerably smaller by comparison to the previous year's program. The FY 1942 warship-building program, which began in mid-1941, included funding to construct two carriers, two light cruisers, sixty destroyers, and 2twenty submarines.

The FY 1942 building program comprises the final appropriation for warship construction in the time period examined in this thesis. The final few pages will be dedicated to a short analysis of events leading up to the attack on Pearl Harbor, followed by an analysis of the causal factors of this phase of the analysis.

Final Steps Toward Entering the War

On 26 July 1941, in response to Japanese incursions in French Indochina, President Roosevelt issued an executive order freezing all Japanese assets within the US and effectively imposed an oil embargo on Japan. Admiral Stark wrote Admiral Kimmell, his commander in the Pacific that "this policy probably involved war in the near future."[41] Upon learning of the embargo, the Japanese estimated their reserves would last between six and twenty-four months.

By August 1941, through transfers from the Pacific, the Atlantic Fleet had grown to include three aircraft carriers, five battleships, and over fifty destroyers and was increasingly capable of countering the U-boat threat.[42] Roosevelt's decision to inaugurate convoy escort operations in the Atlantic was designed to provoke an incident at sea with German U-boats as was alluded to in a forthcoming radio address. On 4 September 1941, he got his wish when a German U-boat torpedoed the destroyer USS *Greer* while operating southwest of Iceland. She managed to limp back to port for repairs and thus avoided a major catastrophe. In a nationwide radio address, President Roosevelt asserted that he had "sought no shooting war with Hitler," but that "American naval vessels . . . will no longer wait until Axis submarines . . . strike their deadly blow--first. ... Our patrolling vessels and planes will protect all merchant ships--not only American ships but ships of any flag--engaged in commerce in our defensive waters."[43] King's reaction was swift with the first US convoy escort action commencing on 16 September, which allowed the Royal Navy escorts to begin withdrawing on the twenty-seventh.

Despite the significant number of warships transferred to him from the Pacific Fleet, Admiral King still did not possess enough to meet his expanding requirements for convoy escorts. His lack of destroyers forced him to overstretch their tactical abilities against a seasoned adversary and began to produce unfortunate results the following month. On 17 October, the destroyer USS *Kearny* (DD 432) was torpedoed and damaged with eleven killed in the vicinity of Iceland. Later that month, the oiler USS *Salinas* (AO 19) was torpedoed and damaged 700 miles off of the coast of Newfoundland. The relative luck of US escorts in surviving these attacks ended on 31 October, when the destroyer USS *Reuben James* (DD 245) was torpedoed and sunk near Iceland with 115 killed. Her loss marked the first US Navy vessel lost in what was to become World War II.

In a Navy Day radio address on 27 October, President Roosevelt, in response to the *Greer*, *Kearny*, and *Salinas* incidents announced that: "America has been attacked." He went on to add that he had issued "orders to the American Navy to shoot on sight, whenever German vessels were encountered."[44] The president was gambling that the American public would not find flaws in his logic which stipulated that warships engaged in convoy operations were due rights of innocent passage. Fortunately, his gamble succeeded and the public was outraged at the incident. Following the loss of the *Reuben James*, the president again used a national radio address to suggest that she was the victim of an unprovoked attack by Germany.

Despite the somewhat "fuzzy: interpretation of the neutrality rights due US warships, the Roosevelt administration's effort to stir public opinion against Germany and in favor of modifying the Neutrality Acts had worked. In a 5 November Gallup poll, 81 percent of those polled favored arming merchant ships and 61 percent favored lifting the restrictions on these ships entering war zones. On 17 November, the president's desired relaxations in the Neutrality Acts were passed and allowed for the arming of US merchantmen and manning these weapons with naval gun crews. Additionally the relaxations allowed US merchant ships to sail into European war zones and to enter belligerent ports for the first time.[45] Ironically, with all the US effort focused on the Atlantic, events in the Pacific were soon to supersede them.

On 25 November, President Roosevelt, while conferring with his principal military and foreign advisors on events in the Pacific, confessed that, "We were likely to be attacked."[46] Ironically on that same day, Admiral Nagumo's six aircraft carriers Pearl Harbor strike force rendezvoused in Tankan Bay in the Kurile Islands and began to steam east towards the Hawaiian Islands.

Through years driven by a series of evolving factors and driven by several key individuals, by 7 December 1941 the US Navy had made such significant strides in warship construction through the previous eight years that the number of warships under construction on the day of the attack on Pearl Harbor actually exceeded the number of warships in the fleet at that time as depicted below in table 4.[47]

Table 4. US Warships on 7 December 1941		
	In Commission	Under Construction
Battleships	17	15
Carriers	7	11
Cruisers	37	54
Destroyers	171	191
Submarines	111	73
Total	**343**	**344**

Causal Factors

The most significant political causal factor of the period from 1940 to 1941 was the fall of France. What had to this point been largely considered a "European war" became something entirely different in the minds of Americans when Britain was left alone to stand against Germany in the summer of 1940. This rapid shift in public sentiment began to play out immediately in the actions of the Congress as it approved two massive increases to the FY 1941 building program in May and July 1940. Just prior to the fall of France, the FY 1941 building program had been approved with funding to construct only twenty-one warships. Attempts to increase the size of the fleet, which had been unsuccessfully lobbied for by a series of secretaries of the Navy suddenly, met with broad approval. Additionally, the fall of France helped to solidify the US relationship with Britain and led to the transfer of destroyers to aid the British cause. As these decommissioned vessels were due to be recommissioned into the US Navy, their transfer induced an increase in the FY 1942 appropriation for destroyers.

The most significant military causal factor of the period from 1940 to 1941 was the evolving perception of a growing likelihood of US military involvement in a war with Germany. Throughout 1940 and 1941 the US Navy increasingly assumed more responsibility in ensuring US goods successfully reached Britain. The US Navy did not possess enough warships to fight a two-ocean war and was forced to ration warships between its two fleets. For most of this phase, the US grew increasingly and solely attuned to events in Europe and anticipates joining the war as an ally of Britain. However, the reduction of the Pacific Fleet to bolster Atlantic assets conveys a signal of weakness to the Japanese which they eventually take advantage of in their attack on Pearl

Harbor. Nonetheless, once France fell, it was plainly clear that the US still did not possess a fleet large enough to meet its needs in the looming war. This event crystallized the military necessity of a rapid expansion of the US Navy.

The most significant economic causal factor of the period from 1940 to 1941 was the removal of all economic constraints on warship construction following the fall of France. Whereas economic pressures had played a significant roll in limiting the size of building appropriations prior to May 1940, once France fell, the concerns over the cost of building warships evaporated in the face of the emergency now facing Britain.

Overall, the most significant causal factor of the phase from 1940 to 1941 was the shift in military perceptions that the fall of France had in producing a massive expansion to the FY 1941 building program. The two expansions to the FY 1941 building program in May and July totaled 322 warships; a massive amount considering the US Navy on 7 December 1941 totaled only 343 warships. In that one key event laid the impetus for the largest expansion in warships the US Navy had ever seen. Ironically, this massive increase in building was inspired by and meant to operate in Europe. When war did come, the ships of the FY 1941 building program would comprise the bulk of the Pacific Fleet who fought back the Japanese through five years of war.

---

[1] V. R. Cardozier, *The Mobilization of the United Stated in World War II: How the Government, Military and Industry Prepared for War* (Jefferson, NC: McFarlane and Company, Inc., 1995), 12.

[2] Ibid., 11.

[3] Ibid., 11.

[4] Robert W. Love Jr., *The History of the U. S. Navy,* vol. 1, *1775-1941* (Harrisonburg, PA: Stackpole Books, 1992), 622.

[5] Ibid., 627.

[6] Edward S. Miller, *War Plan ORANGE* (Annapolis, MD: Naval Institute Press, 1991), 322.

[7] Robert Gardiner, *Conway's All the World's Fighting Ships, 1922-1946* (London: Conway Maritime Press, 1980), 89.

[8] U.S. Naval Expansion Act, 14 June 1940, *Statues at Large* (1939-1941), vol. 54, pt 1.

[9] Ibid.

[10] Paolo E. Colletta, *American Secretaries of the Navy,* vol. 2 (Annapolis, MD: Naval Institute Press, 1980), 678.

[11] Ibid., 678.

[12] Ibid., 679.

[13] Ibid., 677.

[14] Ibid., 682.

[15] Love, 622.

[16] U.S. Naval Expansion Act, 19 July 1940, *Statues at Large* (1939-1941), vol. 54, pt 1.

[17] Ibid

[18] Gardiner, 89.

[19] Ibid., 89.

[20] Colletta, 686.

[21] Ibid., 693.

[22] Ibid., 696.

[23] Ibid., 697.

[24] Ibid., 697.

[25] Ibid., 697.

[26] Gardiner, 270.

[27] Henry H. Adams, *Witness to Power: The Life of Fleet Admiral William D. Leahy* (Annapolis, MD: Naval Institute Press, 1985), 350.

[28] Elliot Roosevelt, ed., *F.D.R. His Personal Letters; 1928-1945,* vols. 1 and 2 (New York, NY: Duell, Sloan and Pearce, 1950), 1049.

[29] Ibid., 1049.

[30] Colletta, 688.

[31] Roosevelt, 1057.

[32] U.S. Destroyers for Bases Agreement, 2 September 1940, *Statues at Large* (1939-1941), vol. 54, pt 2.

[33] Love, 628.

[34] Ibid., 629.

[35] Ibid., 629.

[36] Ibid., 635.

[37] Ibid., 635.

[38] Ibid., 635.

[39] U.S. Lend Lease Act, 11 March 1941, *Statues at Large* (1941-1942), vol. 55, pt 1.

[40] Love, 630.

[41] Ibid., 658.

[42] Ibid., 646.

[43] Ibid., 647.

[44] Ibid., 652.

[45] Ibid., 652.

[46] Ibid., 661.

[47] E. B. Potter, *Sea power: A Naval History* (Annapolis, MD: United States Naval Institute, 1981), 235.

CHAPTER 5

SUMMARY AND CONCLUSION

The attack on Pearl Harbor was one of the darkest days in the US Navy's history. This attack on the Pacific Fleet succeeded in gaining for the Japanese a temporary strategic advantage that enabled them to seize the natural resource-laden areas of the Southwest Pacific. However, on that same morning the US Navy had something of a secret weapon with which to minimize the length of time that Japan held this advantage. Despite sudden and significant losses, the US Navy had a second fleet of warships in various stages of construction and of equal or even greater strength to that which was already in commission. Through a series of evolving factors, the US Congress appropriated funding for 586 warships from 1933 up until the attack. As new efficiencies were adopted in producing this large appropriation of warships, the time spent constructing these new warships continued to decline as the war progressed.

The thesis is that the causal factors which led to the massive prewar warship-building program can be traced to an evolving mix of military, political, and economic issues throughout the years 1933 to 1941. In order to more clearly understand the evolving nature of these factors, the analysis was broken down into three distinct phases. Phase one commenced with the inauguration of President Roosevelt in 1933 and ran through 1937, concluding with the attack on the USS *Panay*. Phase two ran from 1938 through the fall of France in the summer of 1940. Phase three ran from the fall of France until the attack on Pearl Harbor on 7 December 1941.

This thesis analysis began by introducing the post-World War I environment of naval arms limitation treaties such as the Washington Treaty of 1922 where a potentially dangerous naval arms race was prevented by securing tonnage limits on capital warship construction among the world's naval powers. The London Treaty of 1930 extended the tonnage limits to other warships, such as cruisers and destroyers, in order to prevent a naval arms race from taking flight in these classes of previously nonregulated warships. By the early 1930s, the Great Depression had so curtailed the US Navy's warship-building programs that for the four years of the Hoover administration not a single warship had been authorized.

When President Roosevelt came to office in early 1933, he began to implement his New Deal package of economic recovery policies. Fortunately for the Navy, the new president was a recent convert to the Keynesian school of economic thought which advocated deficit spending as a means to extract the country from its slump. Fortunately for Roosevelt, Representative Carl Vinson, the chairman of the House Naval Affairs Committee, took charge of the problem by craftily inserting a significant warship construction program within the massive National Industrial Recovery Act, which contained spending bills for various stimulus projects. Once the shipbuilding industry was rekindled by this injection of government spending on capital improvements, the annual warship-building programs began to see steady annual appropriations through the end of the phase. Despite a widespread pacifist and isolationist sentiment within America during this time frame, Vinson was able to consistently get the appropriations bills through Congress due to his emphasis on the economic stimulus potential of warship construction.

Although both the Washington and London treaties set maximums on the US Fleet, neither played a significant role in shaping warship construction programs, as the

US did not fully fund a treaty-sized fleet until after the collapse of the treaty system. The principal war plan at the time, War Plan Orange, was predicated on employment of a treaty-sized fleet by the US. But as these numbers were never achieved until just prior to World War II, its influence on warship construction cannot be considered significant.

Therefore, the most significant causal factor of the US Navy's warship-building program during this first phase of analysis was the economic benefit associated with funding warship construction. Since it was widely held that 85 percent of all funds spent for construction would go directly to labor, warship construction was congressionally supported as an effective means to stimulate economic recovery, despite its politically unpopular aspects of actually producing warships. Taking into consideration the prevalent pacifist mood of America during this time and the acceptance of diminished naval power, the economic influence of warship construction represents the most significant causal factor of the phase. Although relatively moderate in size, (see table 1),[1] these appropriations established a steady pace of construction, where none had existed for the four years previous to 1933 and maintained it throughout the first phase of the analysis.

Table 5. Warship Building Appropriations: 1933-1937						
Phase 1						
	FY 34	NIRA	FY 35	FY 36	FY 37	Total
CV		2		1		3
BB						0
CA		1	4			5
CL		4	3	2		9
DD	4	20	14	14	12	64
SS		4	6	6	6	22
Total	5	30	27	23	18	103

During phase two of the analysis, the treaty system had all but collapsed following Japan's withdrawal from the Second London Conference. The architecture that had successfully capped the size of the world's navies since 1922 no longer existed as a realistic restriction following Japan's withdrawal. US suspicion of Japan, already heightened following her attack on the USS *Panay,* was further elevated with her commencement of an aggressive warship-building program meant to close the now abandoned treaty-mandated warship gap with the US. Despite significant concerns with Japan, rapidly unfolding events in Europe began to displace Japan as the most pressing international issue for the US. The evolution of the new German state from nationalism to militarism to threat to European security was not immediately recognized and led to the 1938 appeasement of Hitler at Munich.

As the threat of a European war once again became more likely, the US began to take steps to prepare to assist its allies and to ensure American commerce could transit the oceans unmolested. The Atlantic Squadron was created from assets diverted from the Pacific and began to patrol the approaches along the East Coast. Despite the increasingly alarming situations in both Asia and Europe, domestic politics continued to be dominated by isolationists and pacifists. The US Navy was, in the words of Admiral Stark, "not now fully prepared,"[2] to fight a war in either ocean, but faced a scenario where it might be called on to fight in either one, or both. In order to combat this readiness crisis, the US Navy had to try to enlarge its warship building programs without raising the ire of a public who overwhelmingly were against US involvement in the war.

Therefore the most significant causal factor behind the warship building of this second phase was the increasing military threat brought on by the rearmament of both

Japan and Germany. Although the leadership within the US Navy was increasingly aware of the growing threat to US interests posed by a rearmed Japan and Germany, these sentiments were not shared by the public or the Congress and thus did not result in any real increases in numbers of warships funded. Although the overall number of warships appropriated during this phase was somewhat modest, the numbers of capital ships built throughout the phase were significant. Further, these warships, appropriated during phase two (see table 2),[3] constituted a good deal of those that were either in commission on 7 December 1941 and were destined to play a significant role in the opening phases of the war. Due to the time required to construct warships, appropriating these ships during phase two meant that they would be available during the most desperate early phases of the Pacific War. Without their additions to the fleet, the US Navy may not have been capable of halting the Japanese expansion through the South Pacific in 1942.

Table 6.	Warship Building Appropriations: 1938-1940				
	FY 38	FY 39	FY 40	FY 41	Total
CV		1		1	2
BB	2	2	2	2	8
CA					0
CL	2	2	2	2	8
DD	16		8	8	32
SS	8		8	8	24
Total	28	5	20	21	74

With France's unexpected fall to the Germans, Britain was left to stand alone in a much more ominous environment. This emergency virtually eliminated America's previously strong domestic influences of isolationism and pacifism, which had served to constrain the US Navy's warship building program up until the fall of France. Even before France surrendered, the FY 1941 building program was dramatically expanded by over four times its initial size when in May 1940, the program was expanded to include a further ninety-four warships. Immediately thereafter the Naval Expansion Acts of May and July 1940 raised the ceilings on allowable warship tonnage and created even more space for expansion. These increases in allowable tonnage were quickly filled both in the May 1940 expansions to the FY 1841 building program and a further expansion in July which included the funding for construction of 228 additional warships. Thus, in a matter of just a few months, the US Navy transitioned from a steady state building program to one greatly expanded to match evolving wartime requirements.

There is no doubt that the most significant causal factor of this third phase of warship production was the clear military requirements for the US to bolster Britain against the Axis onslaught. Pacifism and isolationism, which had served to limit warship building programs in the past, held no credence after the fall of France. Military prudence and combat expectations drove the massive building programs (see table 3),[4] to quantities unseen in the history of the US Navy. The appropriations of May and July 1940 are of particular interest since the ships produced under these programs constituted the bulk of the fleet that fought and won the war in the Pacific.

Table 7.	Warship Building Appropriations: 1940-1941			
	Phase 3			
	May-40	Jul-40	FY 42	Total
CV	6	4	2	12
BB	2	5		7
CA	4	6		10
CL	9	25	2	36
DD	45	151	60	256
SS	28	37	23	88
Total	94	228	87	409

Interpretations of the Most Significant Causal Factor for Period 1933-1941

Table 8^5 depicts the total warship appropriations by phase, for the entire period of this analysis and is useful in determining the most significant causal factor for the entire period.

Table 8.	Warship Building Appropriations: 1933-1941			
	Warship Appropriations (1933-1941)			
	Phase 1	Phase 2	Phase 3	Total
CV	3	2	12	17
BB	0	8	7	15
CA	5	0	10	15
CL	9	8	36	53
DD	64	32	256	352
SS	22	24	88	134
Total	103	74	409	586

As discussed above and in the previous chapters, the significant causal factor of each phase evolved as events unfolded through the years. In phase one, the recognized economic benefits inherent in warship construction served to drive funding for the annual programs despite an environment of fiscal austerity. In phase two, military preparedness began to drive building programs, but was restrained by domestic political and economic agendas. In phase three, these restrictive domestic restraints on military spending evaporated following the fall of France and the loss of a key ally whose resources had been integrated into US and British war plans. As table 8 depicts, 70 percent of all warships funded throughout the entire period occurred in phase three. The warships funded in phase three depict the majority of the US Navy that was to fight and win in the Pacific during World War II.

Applications of Lessons Learned from the Analysis

The irony behind the increase in funding during phase three is that the impetus behind this dramatic surge in building occurred in Europe, where the US initially expected to employ the bulk of its navy in supporting its sole remaining ally, Britain against the Axis. Fortunately for the US, the mix of warships constructed as well as their inherent adaptability enabled them to successfully operate in the Pacific Ocean as well as the Atlantic against both the Japanese and the Germans. There are several lessons to be drawn from this period that can be applicable to the US Navy today. These lessons can be grouped into two main categories; those that suggest caution and those that suggest hope regarding warship building in today's environment.

From a cautionary aspect, the study of warship production during the period 1933 through 1941, cautions that the US no longer possess the ability to mass produce warships on the eve of war as was done just prior to World War II. With reduced numbers of operating shipyards in the United States along with the increased complexity of modern warships, it is simply unreasonable to expect a rapid throughput production increase in support of a massive prewar rearmament. Additionally, as all this involves time, it can be assumed that the nation's potential adversaries are also aware of its limitations in production and that it would be expected that they would not afford the US the luxury of the time necessary to build up to wartime requirements.

Over the past decades, the cost of ship construction within the US has increased so significantly over the rest of the world that virtually no commercial shipbuilding occurs in the US. As a result most of the nation's shipyards have been forced to close as business has moved overseas to cheaper markets, such as South Korea. At present there are five shipyards constructing warships which are kept steadily busy by the modest annual building programs of the US Navy and a few other smaller yards supporting routine maintenance to the fleet. The country possesses limited excess capacity necessary to increase its warship fleet in the event of war.

The increased complexity of modern warships also limits the production efficiencies that could be expected should the fleet need to rapidly expand in the event of war. Modern US warships have the most advanced propulsion, weapons, and sensor systems afloat. Modern submarine hulls are constructed with exotic alloys, which require special handling and welding techniques. Further, bith aircraft carriers and submarines are nuclear powered and require significant safety oversights to safely install and operate these plants; all of which increases construction time. Additionally, modern warships increasingly incorporate stealth and signature reduction technologies, which also increase construction time necessary for manufacture and installation.

Finally, it is unlikely, given the US's relatively dominant military strength, that a potential adversary would conduct an attack against the US which allow the navy sufficient time to fund and construct a significant warship building program. Given the time necessary to fund and build warships, it is far more likely that an enemy would conduct his war in such a manner as to limit the US's ability to make use of time to increase its fleet size.

The hopeful lessons to be drawn from the US Navy's warship-building program of 1933 through 1941 include the example that the Navy needs to avail itself of every opportunity available to facilitate warship construction in peacetime. As was the case in late 1941, the Navy's steady peacetime pursuit of a robust and well-balanced fleet has historically served it well upon the outbreak of hostilities.

As during the mid-to-late 1930s it is sometime hard to draw attention to a specific threat that warrants increases in spending on warship construction. Frequently, in a peacetime environment, the funds to finance annual building programs are earmarked for other programs, sometime with higher domestic political backing. As with some of the early building initiatives prior to World War II, the Navy needs to be aware of the confluence of interests which encompass a building program and continue to maximize their political potential. The nation's limited shipyards are seen as a diminishing strategic asset and as such are kept alive through annual warship-building programs. These same yards support the economic viability of their local communities and the tradesmen employed therein and as such engender political support to keep them open and busy. The warship-building program of 1933-1941 availed itself of these many interests to get through Congress programs which otherwise may not have been appropriated, and that philosophy continues to have merit today.

Following the attack on Pearl Harbor, the fleet that was in commission, regardless of the factors that led to each ship's construction, went to war and played a significant role in halting the Japanese aggression in the Pacific. Therefore, in peacetime, it will always be a challenge to fund warship construction to levels deemed necessary by the Navy. Programs will frequently be trimmed by competition for limited dollars. Regardless of these frustrations, building must be pursued, as it is likely to be too late to act on the need once war has broken out.

The US Navy's warship-building programs for the past several decades have taken the previous lesson to heart. The Navy has continued steadily to construct warships in peacetime, so that the capacity is readily available in time of crisis. In all of the nation's wars over the past four decades, the Navy has been able to meet tasking without having to drastically increase its building programs because it has taken steadily constructed warships on an annual basis during peacetime. The US Navy of the past several decades, although increasingly smaller in numbers of warships, has been increasingly enlarged in terms of lethality due to the increased modernity and balance of the fleet. As a testament to the success of the Navy's program of annual peacetime building programs, the fleet of warships in commission at the outbreak of any of the nation's conflicts over the past four decades has been sufficient to meet the requirements of that conflict without significant increases in building.

Therefore, the most significant application of these lessons to today's Navy is the tremendous importance of peacetime warship construction in order to ensure wartime preparedness. Although warships are increasingly expensive and difficult to justify in peacetime, the effort undertaken to appropriate funding for warships in peacetime more than justifies itself at the outbreak of hostilities. In order to maximize the funding for warships in peacetime, the Navy must continue to seek out groups of constituencies who favor warship construction for reasons beyond the military benefit. By creatively pooling the lobbying potential and combined political clout of all the interested parties, the Navy should continue to be successful in funding the construction of a wartime fleet during times of peace. In doing so, the Navy can ensure that a significant wartime capability exists prior to the outbreak of a war and therefore can guarantee that the lessons learned from the pre-World War II buildup have not been lost.

Recommended Further Study

Topics related to this thesis may be expanded into works of their own. Subjects that may prove fruitful to further examination included a study of the results of warship-building programs which garnered legislative support primarily due to their nonmilitary benefits. It would be useful to quantify the military impact of warships funded due to their economic or political benefits. Additionally, further analysis of the causal factors of warship building in today's environment of the Global War on Terror may prove useful, in that the Navy has played a reduced role in this conflict, yet continues to build warships. It would be beneficial to trace the shift in causal factors throughout the years following World War II, through the Cold War, and beyond. Additionally, a thorough study of individuals who played a major role in the pre-World War II buildup, such as Representative Vinson, President Roosevelt, or Secretary Knox, would certainly be beneficial to the understanding of the era.

---

[1]Robert Gardiner, *Conway's All the World's Fighting Ships, 1922-1946* (London: Conway Maritime Press, 1980), 88.

[2]Robert W. Love Jr., *The History of the U. S. Navy,* vol. 1, *1775-1941* (Harrisonburg, PA: Stackpole Books, 1992), 612.

[3] Gardiner, 88.

[4] Ibid., 89.

[5] Ibid., 89.

BIBLIOGRAPHY

Adams, Henry H. *Witness to Power: The Life of Fleet Admiral William D. Leahy.* Annapolis, MD: Naval Institute Press, 1985.

Brinkley, Alan. *The End of Reform; New Deal Liberalism in Recession and War.* New York, NY: Alfred A. Knopf, 1995.

Cardozier, V. R. *The Mobilization of the United Stated in World War II: How the Government, Military and Industry Prepared for War.* Jefferson, NC: McFarlane and Company, Inc., 1995.

Colletta, Paolo E. *American Secretaries of the Navy.* Vol. 2. Annapolis, MD: Naval Institute Press, 1980.

Connery, Robert H. *The Navy and the Industrial Mobilization in World War II.* Princeton, NJ: Princeton University Press, 1951.

Cooling, Benjamin F., and Allison W. Saville. *War, Business, and American Society: Historical Perspectives on the Military-Industrial Complex.* Port Washington, NY: National University Publications, 1977.

Dallek, Robert. *Franklin D. Roosevelt and American Foreign Policy, 1932-1945.* New York, NY: Oxford University Press, 1979.

Davis, Kenneth S. *FDR, Into the Storm, 1937-1940.* New York, NY: Random House, 1993.

Earle, Edward M., ed. *Makers of Modern Strategy; Military Thought from Machiavelli to Hitler.* Princeton, NJ: Princeton University Press, 1971.

Fassett, F. G., ed. *The Shipbuilding Business in the United States of America.* Vols. 1 and 2. New York, NY: The Society of Naval Architects and Marine Engineers, 1948.

Furer, Julius A. *Administration of the Navy Department in World War II.* Washington, DC: U.S. Government Printing Office, 1959.

Gardiner, Robert. *Conway's All the World's Fighting Ships, 1922-1946.* London: Conway Maritime Press, 1980.

Gilbert, Martin. *First World War Atlas.* NewYork, NY: The Macmillan Company, 1970.

Gole, Henry G. *The Road to Rainbow.* Annapolis, MD: Naval Institute Press, 2003.

Heinrichs, Waldo. *Threshold of War.* New York, NY: Oxford University Press, 1988.

Lane, Fredrick C. *Ships for Victory A History of Shipbuilding under the U.S. Maritime*

Commission in World War II. Baltimore, MD: The Johns Hopkins Press, 1951.

Leahy, William D. *I Was There*. New York, NY: Whittlesey House Publishing Co., 1950.

Leuchtenburg, William E. *Franklin D. Roosevelt and the New Deal: 1932-1940*. New York, NY: Harper and Row Publishing Co. 1963.

Love, Robert W. Jr. *The History of the U. S. Navy.* Vol. 1, *1775-1941*. Harrisonburg, PA: Stackpole Books, 1992.

Marolda, Edward J., ed. *FDR and the U.S. Navy*. New York, NY: St. Martin's Press, 1998.

McBride, William M. "The unstable dynamics of a strategic technology: Disarmament, unemployment, and the interwar battleship." *Technology and Culture* 38, no. 2, (April 1997): 386-424.

McKercher, B. J. C., ed. *Arms Limitations and Disarmament: Restraints on War, 1918-1939*. London: Praeger Publishing, 1992.

McMurtrie, Francis E. *Jane's Fighting Ships, 1943-4*. New York, NY: MacMillan Co., 1945.

Miller, Edward S. *War Plan Orange*. Annapolis, MD: Naval Institute Press, 1991.

Mitchell, Donald W. *History of the Modern American Navy, From 1883 through Pearl Harbor*. New York, NY: Alfred A Knopf, 1946.

Morison, Samuel Elliot. *The Two-Ocean War: A Short History of the United States Navy in the Second World War.* Boston, MA: Little, Brown and Company, 1963.

Potter, E. B. *Admiral Arleigh Burke*. New York, NY: Random House, 1990.

Potter, E. B. *Sea Power: A Naval History*. Annapolis, MD: United States Naval Institute, 1981.

Roberts, Stephen S. "U.S. Navy Building Programs During World War II." *Warship International* 13, no. 3 (1981): 218-261.

Roosevelt, Elliot. ed. *F.D.R. His Personal Letters; 1928-1945*. Vols. 1 and 2. New York, NY: Duell, Sloan, and Pearce, 1950.

Roskill, Stephen W. *Naval Policy Between the Wars.* New York, NY: Walker and Company, 1968.

Simpson, B. Mitchell, III, ed. *The Development of Naval Theory: Essays by Herbert Rosinski*. Newport, RI: Naval War College Press, 1977.

Thompson, Robert S. *A Time for War: Franklin Delano Roosevelt and the Path to Pearl Harbor*. New York, NY: Prentice Hall Press, 1991.

Tuleja, Thadeus V. *Statesmen and Admirals*. New York, NY: W. W. Norton and Company, Inc., 1963.

U.S. Destroyers for Bases Agreement. *Statues at Large* 54 (1940).

U.S. Lend Lease Act. *Statues at Large* 55 (1941)

U.S. Naval Arms Limitation Treaty, 6 February 1922. *Statues at Large* (1923-1925), vol. 43, pt 2.

U.S. Naval Armament Limitation Treaty, 22 April 1930. *Statues at Large* (1929-1931), vol. 46, pt 2.

U.S. Naval Armament Multilateral, 25 March 1936. *Statues at Large* (1937), vol. 50, pt 2.

U.S. Naval Expansion Act, 14 June 1940. *Statues at Large* (1939-1941), vol. 54, pt 1.

U.S. Naval Expansion Act, 19 July 1940. *Statues at Large* (1939-1941), vol. 54, pt 1.

"US Navy Active Ship Force Levels, 1917-Present." Database on-line. Washington DC: U.S. Naval Historical Center. Accessed 24 September 2004. Available from http://www.history.navy.mil/branches/org9-4.htm. Internet.

Whitehurst, Clinton H., Jr. *The U.S. Shipbuilding Industry: Past, Present and Future*. Annapolis, MD: Naval Institute Press: 1986.

INITIAL DISTRIBUTION LIST

Combined Arms Research Library
U.S. Army Command and General Staff College
250 Gibbon Ave.
Fort Leavenworth, KS 66027-2314

Defense Technical Information Center/OCA
825 John J. Kingman Rd., Suite 944
Fort Belvoir, VA 22060-6218

Lieutenant Colonel Marian E. Vlasak
Combat Studies Institute
USACGSC
1 Reynolds Ave.
Fort Leavenworth, KS 66027-1352

Dr. Stephen D. Coats
DJMO
USACGSC
1 Reynolds Ave.
Fort Leavenworth, KS 66027-1352

Mr. David W. Christie
DJMO
USACGSC
1 Reynolds Ave.
Fort Leavenworth, KS 66027-1352

CERTIFICATION FOR MMAS DISTRIBUTION STATEMENT

1. Certification Date: 17 June 2005

2. Thesis Author: LCDR John M. Barrett, USN

3. Thesis Title: An Analysis of the Causal Factors Behind the United States Navy's Warship-Building Program from 1933 to 1941

4. Thesis Committee Members: _____
   Signatures: _____
   _____

5. Distribution Statement: See distribution statements A-X on reverse, then circle appropriate distribution statement letter code below:

(A) B C D E F X   SEE EXPLANATION OF CODES ON REVERSE

If your thesis does not fit into any of the above categories or is classified, you must coordinate with the classified section at CARL.

6. Justification: Justification is required for any distribution other than described in Distribution Statement A. All or part of a thesis may justify distribution limitation. See limitation justification statements 1-10 on reverse, then list, below, the statement(s) that applies (apply) to your thesis and corresponding chapters/sections and pages. Follow sample format shown below:

EXAMPLE

Limitation Justification Statement	/	Chapter/Section	/	Page(s)
Direct Military Support (10)	/	Chapter 3	/	12
Critical Technology (3)	/	Section 4	/	31
Administrative Operational Use (7)	/	Chapter 2	/	13-32

Fill in limitation justification for your thesis below:

Limitation Justification Statement	/	Chapter/Section	/	Page(s)
_____	/	_____	/	_____
_____	/	_____	/	_____
_____	/	_____	/	_____
_____	/	_____	/	_____
_____	/	_____	/	_____

7. MMAS Thesis Author's Signature: _____

STATEMENT A: Approved for public release; distribution is unlimited. (Documents with this statement may be made available or sold to the general public and foreign nationals).

STATEMENT B: Distribution authorized to U.S. Government agencies only (insert reason and date ON REVERSE OF THIS FORM). Currently used reasons for imposing this statement include the following:

    1. Foreign Government Information. Protection of foreign information.

    2. Proprietary Information. Protection of proprietary information not owned by the U.S. Government.

    3. Critical Technology. Protection and control of critical technology including technical data with potential military application.

    4. Test and Evaluation. Protection of test and evaluation of commercial production or military hardware.

    5. Contractor Performance Evaluation. Protection of information involving contractor performance evaluation.

    6. Premature Dissemination. Protection of information involving systems or hardware from premature dissemination.

    7. Administrative/Operational Use. Protection of information restricted to official use or for administrative or operational purposes.

    8. Software Documentation. Protection of software documentation - release only in accordance with the provisions of DoD Instruction 7930.2.

    9. Specific Authority. Protection of information required by a specific authority.

    10. Direct Military Support. To protect export-controlled technical data of such military significance that release for purposes other than direct support of DoD-approved activities may jeopardize a U.S. military advantage.

STATEMENT C: Distribution authorized to U.S. Government agencies and their contractors: (REASON AND DATE). Currently most used reasons are 1, 3, 7, 8, and 9 above.

STATEMENT D: Distribution authorized to DoD and U.S. DoD contractors only; (REASON AND DATE). Currently most reasons are 1, 3, 7, 8, and 9 above.

STATEMENT E: Distribution authorized to DoD only; (REASON AND DATE). Currently most used reasons are 1, 2, 3, 4, 5, 6, 7, 8, 9, and 10.

STATEMENT F: Further dissemination only as directed by (controlling DoD office and date), or higher DoD authority. Used when the DoD originator determines that information is subject to special dissemination limitation specified by paragraph 4-505, DoD 5200.1-R.

STATEMENT X: Distribution authorized to U.S. Government agencies and private individuals of enterprises eligible to obtain export-controlled technical data in accordance with DoD Directive 5230.25; (date). Controlling DoD office is (insert).